Elder 1

Come, come, whoever you are.
Wanderer, worshiper, lover of leaving,
It doesn't matter.
Ours is not a caravan of despair.
Come, even if you have broken your vows a thousand times.
Come, yet again, come, come.

JELALUDDIN RUMI

ISBN 978-1-7341128-2-5

Editing by Diane Baumer
Book Design by Damonza

FIRST EDITION
Printed in the United States

www.SteveStroud.org
www.LaraHovda.com

What a delightful departure from many of the
self-help tomes floating about the universe.

—SUZANNE MACPHERSON

Lara and Steve managed to bring fresh insight to a foundational topic breathing life into the journey of self-discovery. I am moved by the compassionate loving motivation underlying the entirety of the book. I honor the knowledge and experience of both of these guides and feel fortunate that such wisdom has been offered to us through the precious result of this writing. I wish to humbly acknowledge that without the kindness, support and patience of people like this the courage to take the journey of self-discovery might not come as easily to fruition. This Mini manual is a must read for everyone and anyone who wonders if they've ever been lost in their wandering but now can learn how the wondering actually is the working.

—STORMIE GRACE PhD

Steve Stroud and Lara Hovda provide an essential roadmap for the contemporary person struggling with overwhelm and feeling lost in finding their authentic balance. The material is easy to digest, provides simple and powerful steps in improving self-awareness and self-compassion, and points the way to finding more truth in oneself. I highly recommend Discovery – from anyone just starting on a path of self-discovery to the seasoned seeker wanting to ensure they cover all their bases.

—JOHN WEPNER, MA, LCMHCA
BRENNAN INTEGRATION PRACTITIONER
PATHWORK HELPER
NATIONAL CERTIFIED COUNSELOR (NCC)

TABLE OF CONTENTS

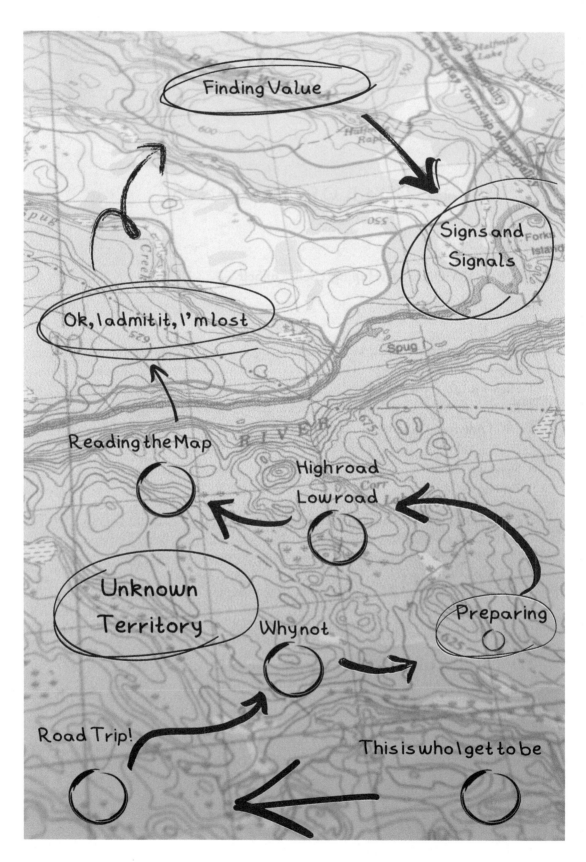

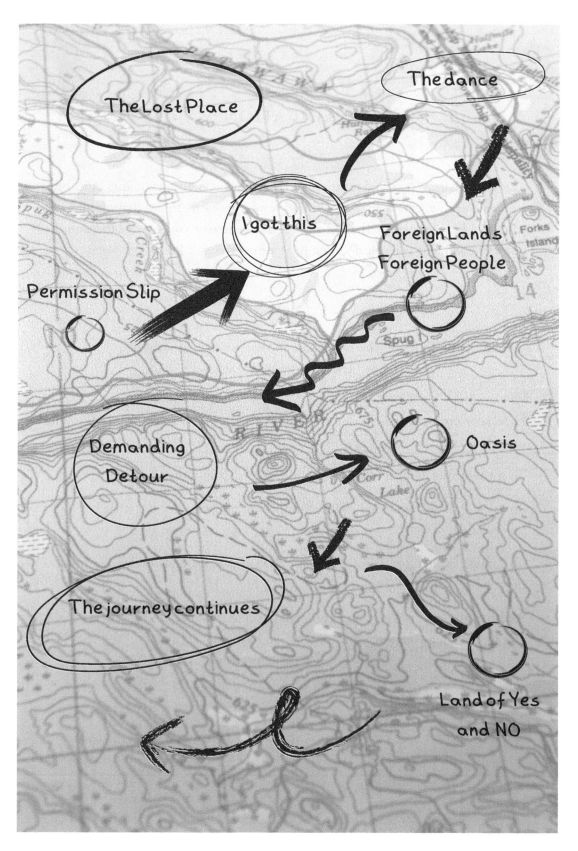

DEDICATION

This book shares a personal journey, and as all journeys go it is unique in its own way. And as all journeys go, you will find some common ground that resonates in your own life experience. There is a good chance that as you wander through the book you will find yourself nodding in agreement- Yea- I know that place.

Steve

To those who have loved me when I have stumbled
and to those who have found me when I was lost.

Especially my wife, Carrie, for your resilience, guidance, companionship, and unending love.

To my daughter, Crystal, for being your beautiful inspirational courageous self.

To my grandkids, Tejah and Ziven, for opening my heart beyond what I thought was possible.

To Annie, Karsten, Jonah and Molly for allowing me the daily practice of becoming my best self.

And to Lara, my co-writer and companion on this journey of Discovery- thank you for bringing your voice and your vision to this adventure.

Lara

This book was written during a time when I needed a map. I had lost the certainty I thought would be there forever. I disappeared and was lost. Since I didn't have a map, I helped create one (A huge thank you to Steve). Even though the path was not always clear and I fell or hid in a hole - A LOT- I took the steps forward through unknown territory back to me. My feeling of home. My True Self.

This Discovery was written for all the women in my life who were there along the way to pack my heart full of acknowledgement, empathy, love and fortitude. Then they would hug me and remind me that it's just about one step at a time and send me on my way.

Thank you, Marion, Nissa, Sarah Z., Mira, Sue, Katya and Maija

AND the reason I found the bravery to go on the journey in the first place

Alia and Ella

INTRODUCTION

When I was young my family would take road trips, we always used a service AAA provided, the TripTik.

We would tell them where our trip would start and where we wanted to go. They would then print out and bind a TripTik. Each page had a small segment of the road visible and if you followed the road on each page you would get to your destination. It was a book of your journey from home to your destination.

I used to sit in the back seat and use a highlighter moving it along the road slowly as the car moved down the highway. Like a really old fashioned GPS. I would look out the window and read each sign to let me know where I was on the map.

This is your TripTik. This is your journey. Each chapter reveals a destination along your journey to the true self.

What is the True Self you may ask? It's feeling at home with yourself. It's a feeling of secure knowing that you can travel through life's windy roads without too many detours.

This is a map of how to connect the dots from cheese stick wrappers on the floor to patience. From the shame of being late to a calm apology. From saying 'yes' too many times to saying 'no' because you need to. From an argument about finances to a response that is insightful and respectful.

We believe in you. We know that each of the stops along the way are part of a larger scaffolding for self care, self love, coming home to the true self.

This is your road map to your true self.

Travel Well,

Steve & Lara

DEVELOPING A SENSE OF SELF

PROLOGUE

A FRIEND ALONG THE WAY

Note to a friend:

I will be joining you in this journey.

A friend is someone who understands the small nuances of what it means to be in self-doubt, pain, or frustration.

On this journey, I'll be here to hold your hand, to show understanding, to support you and even push a little bit.

What I'm asking as you step forward on this journey is to trust yourself.

Know that you are in the exact right space, at the right time, in the right moment.

I'm so proud you are taking care of yourself.

You are EXACTLY where you need to be.

1

ROAD TRIP!

You can't use an old map to explore a new world.

ALBERT EINSTEIN

Note to a friend:

Okay here's the deal, my friend, I don't know what I'm talking about AND I know everything that I want to say. My life is not happening how I planned. Sure, I have elements I wanted. A home. A grown-up job. Kids—no, I actually wanted kids and they are a joy, sometimes. A partner who would love me and give me attention. But, man, there are a lot of blurry lines right now. A LOT of tiredness and a lot of confusion and I need some direction. Do you know what I'm saying?

Do you want to clarify things?

Do you want to create a place where you matter?

Do you want to make healthy choices?

How about resilience? How about some of that?

Well, here you are, and here I am and let's crush this journey together.

Be seeing you along the way.

IF YOU HAVE ever felt lost, wondering how you ended up where you are, or felt that somehow you have misplaced your sense of self or your way, then this is the guidebook for you.

This book is a place to explore undiscovered territories. Discovery- A Road Map to Your True Self is a supportive guided journey that gives you an opportunity to come home to your True Self.

Your True Self is the place where you are so comfortable, known, held, loved, and recognized. It's a place where you tell yourself the truth. Where you are true and authentic.

Is it easy to get there or be there? NOPE. That's why we wrote a book about the journey it takes to find it. I-T. A journey to your True Self. At home, inside of you.

This journey will get you from shaky to solid, from not OK to OK, from feeling unworthy to finding your value and your voice.

This Road Map is so valuable that it will become your new "go-to toolbox." It's full of ideas, directions, interactive exercises, and superpowers that will support you in centering, focusing, and coming back to yourself, again and again.

This Road Map, as with any map, will help you find your way and guide you from where you are to where you long to be—Your True Self.
This journey will guide you through the rich territory of self-discovery and deliver you to your desired destination (YOU!). As you discover your gifts, strengths, and happiness this road map turns into a treasure map. One where you confidently embrace your newfound sense of self.

Your True Self is a place where you live your truth.

This Road Map will guide you through both familiar and new territory. You will come across some amazing vista points, a few rest stops, and of course some construction zones —all necessary aspects of any rewarding adventure. There will even be opportunities to get off the beaten track to explore the bumpy, windy, potholed back roads, taking you to places you have never ventured before.

So where do you start? Simply said, and as true with any venture, you start with where you are. Just like those big maps at the mall with the red dot that states YOU ARE HERE.

This journey starts with where you are—perhaps further from your true self than you would like. Maybe it starts with you feeling not OK about yourself. Maybe it starts with your family not really hearing and valuing what you have to say. Maybe it starts with wanting to ask for help but not knowing how.

But wherever your "YOU ARE HERE" dot may be, this journey will give you the guidance and reassurance needed to find solid ground, know your worth, and use your voice with confidence. The destination then becomes clear—it's your strength, freedom, and finally finding your True Self.

Every journey is simultaneously a beginning and an ending: I was leaving my old life behind and starting on a road trip to find a new me.

Debi Tolbert Duggar

Let's start the journey.

2

WHY NOT

For true success ask yourself these four questions:

Why? Why not? Why not me? Why not now?

JAMES ALLEN

YOU MIGHT ASK, "WHY is this journey important?"

Will it be worth the work?

If we said you were going to get your life back, how would you feel? Scared? Excited? Skeptical? All the above?

On the other side of a storm is the strength that comes from having navigated through it. Raise your sail and begin.

Gregory S. Williams

Fair enough, these are common feelings we all get before setting out on a big trip to unknown places.

What if we told you there is resilience at the end? Or that you could freely love and be loved? Or that, even when everything around you is not OK, somehow in the midst of it all, you discover that you can be OK.

So, good question, "WHY is this journey important?"

THE ANSWER

- To get your life back. Or find a life you have only dreamt about.
- To have the resilience to be OK even when things around you are not OK.
- To freely love and be able to accept love.

As you can see, this is more than a how-to book. It's a journey. A quest, if you will, into the very nature of your True Self and the known and unknown potential that resides within you.

By embarking on this adventure, you will:

- Broaden your awareness.
- Discover mindfulness (Being aware of your needs. I'm hungry and will deal with this meeting better if I had some food in my system).
- Find the courage to transform a part of your life (Green juice - salad - "I am enough." - HERE I COME!).
- Create a life of healthy choices.
- Find your breath when tense (Grr, your daughter just missed her curfew again).
- Find your NO! (I can't do any more work tonight. I don't have the brain power).
- Find your YES! (I would love to go on a walk by the beach with you) because that is what *you* authentically need at the moment.
- Find enough self-compassion to give yourself a time-out (an extra ten minutes in the shower or reading your favorite book).
- Find the ability to put yourself first, not last. (Without guilt!) (Yes, mom's and dad's we see you).

This journey you are starting is about empowered mindful interactions, also known as honest, open communication.

These are just some of the superpowers that you will discover along the way.

Note to a friend:

I know that whole list sounds really awesome and ideal—are you dreaming? I might think, "'I can't become all of that!" Sounds amazing, but really?

Please remember that even if you find one of these things inside of you, you have won the lotto! Just one more bit of self-compassion or allowing yourself to breathe. That breath is your superpower. It's worth considering. You are worth this journey.

I will be right here the whole way reminding you that it's just one breath at a time or just one "Yes" or "No." Or maybe reminding you that you have a friend.

Take the step. It will be SO worth it.

3

PREPARING FOR THE JOURNEY

The journey of a thousand miles begins with one step.

LAO TZU

AS WITH ANY adventure it's best to prepare wisely. Here are a few things that will aid you on your way:

#1 A willingness to participate

Since you have signed up, we assume you are willing. However, it's useful to remember that your desire and willingness to participate will be challenged at times; those construction zones can be frustrating.

#2 A sense of humor

It will serve you well, and it will be much appreciated by those around you.

#3 New eyes

Your motto for the adventure comes from the French novelist Marcel Proust:

> *"The real voyage of discovery consists not in seeking*
> *new lands but seeing with new eyes."*

You may feel as though you are at a crossroads. It's not the first time, and it won't be the last. But now you have this Road Map, and it's time to use it. You're courageous and strong, you have come this far; together, we can start this journey, and you will reach your destination.

Now for just a couple other points of interest: What to pack in your bag for your journey:

> **The goal is not that all things be OK, But to learn how to be OK with all things.**

#1 A journal.

This can be a paper journal or a blank document on a device. This journal is an essential part of the program. Not only does it get all your words, thoughts, and feelings out in front of yous, but it will also give you a reference.

#2 Time.

We know that you are already stretched. But please consider that a few moments you allow for yourself allows you to be there in a much better way for your partner, your children, family, and work. Give this to yourself. Most lessons only take a few minutes to read or listen to. Each action task is maybe 10+ minutes but once you have engaged in this program you will be able to take these tools out into the world and use them for the benefit of all, especially yourself.

A Few Handy Reminders

1. It's valuable to keep in mind that your goal is not that all things will be OK, but that you will have a solid sense of self and the tools to be OK with all things.

2. It's valuable to keep in mind that this transformation will require faith and heartfelt effort.

3. It's valuable to keep in mind that you deserve what you desire:

    -   a seat at the table and a voice

    -   self-compassion

    -   the ability to respond to your own needs

    -   the freedom to be just who you are and still be loved

> **When you get stranded, the way to start moving again is not to search for an answer, but to find a new question to which your life can be the answer.**
>
> **Jennifer Krause**

So, let's get started.

Let's open the map and get an overview of the terrain before us.

One of the first things you will see is that there are 18 territories in your Road Map. Each of the territories will offer you the opportunity to explore your superpowers. This format will guide you through your journey.

Selfcompassion

Superpower

4

HIGHER ROAD – LOWER ROAD

*It is our choices, Harry, that show what we truly
are, far more than our abilities.*

J.K. ROWLING

AS YOU TRAVEL through this journey, you will see that at each crossroads, off-ramp, or intersection you have the option to take the Higher Road or the Lower Road.

Characteristics of the Higher Road include patience, compassion, understanding, forgiveness, and connection.

The Lower Road characteristics are the familiar territories of feeling misunderstood, blame, frustration, living and reliving painful patterns.

In reality, we are always a combination of both the Higher and the Lower Roads.

> **The path isn't a straight line; it's a spiral. You continually come back to the things you thought you understood and see deeper truths.**
>
> **- Barry H. Gillespie**

As you travel through your journey you will find the treasures and the awareness that will allow you to use what is perhaps the greatest of superpowers—choice. You will learn that you can choose to walk that habitual Lower Road or along the Higher Road more and more of the time.

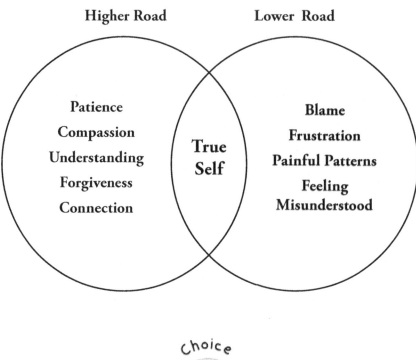

Higher Road   **Lower Road**

Patience

Compassion

Understanding   **True**   Blame

Forgiveness   **Self**   Frustration

Connection   Painful Patterns

Feeling

Misunderstood

Choice

Superpower

5

READING THE MAP

I wisely started with a map.

J.R.R. TOLKIEN (*THE HOBBIT*)

The Landscape

To follow a map, it's best to be familiar with the symbols and language of the map.

The Map

Let's start with exploring some of the symbols and language you will come across in your journey. The idea here is to flush out what a particular word or concept means for you. This is valuable because what you understand a particular word or concept to mean may be different from what someone else understands it to mean.

Take, for example, the word "freedom." The Oxford Languages Dictionary definition is "the right to act, speak, or think as one wants without restraint". Now, wouldn't that be great? Just to be free. But what does "freedom" mean to you specifically? What does it look like and how would it feel to be "free" from whatever is tying you down? The idea here is that if you want to experience freedom, you need to define what it means for you. What does "freedom" look like for you?

The idea here is that the more clearly you define a particular word or concept, the more clearly you can communicate and create it.

This is true for any word or concept that you will come across in your journey.

> **The more clearly you define a particular word or concept, the more clearly you can communicate and create it.**

Clarifying what a word or concept means for you enhances your ability to communicate your wants and needs and to connect to others with more understanding.

The Road Ahead

Let's pick a few words and flush out their meaning. We have defined these from the dictionary, but the idea is to see what your felt understanding of the word or concept is. There is no right or wrong, just clarification. You can always add to the list but let's start with these.

Road Signs

Authentic—true to one's own personality, spirit, or character.

Automatic Writing—ability to understand something immediately, without the need for conscious reasoning. Automatic Writing allows you to see your intuition in a physical form. It is a tool that makes your intuition concrete.

Awareness—knowledge and understanding that something is happening or exists.

Body-Mind Connection—your mind affects your body, and your body affects your mind.

Choice—to have the freedom and power to select one thing but reject another.

Construction Zone—a section of each chapter that contains experientials. Here you have a chance to slow down and put into practice the concepts of the course.

Doer—someone who navigates through life from an action-oriented perspective.

Demands—anytime you *insist* someone, or something *must* be a certain way (as opposed to a True Need).

Empower—to give official authority; to promote the self-actualization or influence of.

Feeler—someone who navigates through life from a sensitive, intuitive, emotional, and feeling perspective.

Lost—unable to find one's way; not knowing one's whereabouts.

Mundane—the ordinary things you do every day—the dishes, the laundry, driving kids around.

Neutral—engagement without attachment; a position of awareness and philosophy.

Overwhelm—completely overcome or overpowered by a thought or a feeling.

Pause—giving yourself a moment to collect yourself.

Permission slip—allowing someone, or yourself, to do a particular thing or be a particular way.

Presence—living in the moment, i.e., "right now."

Pull—an act of exerting force on someone to cause movement toward oneself.

Push—an act of exerting force on someone to move them forward or away.

Reaction—something done on impulse, without considering what the result may be.

Response—something done with thoughtful awareness as to how actions affect outcomes.

Self-Worth—a feeling that you are a good person who deserves to be treated with respect.

Soul-full—the voice that calls you forward. This is the inner voice that whispers hope and courage. That gives you resilience and strength in the toughest of times.

Stop—to prevent an action or event from happening; shut down.

Taking Inventory—checking in with your body, mind, and emotions.

Thinker—someone who navigates through life from an analytical, mental, and thinking perspective.

True Need—A *true need* arises from a place of knowing and listening to your True Self. It is an innate understanding of what is essential to make you materially and spiritually happy, holy, healthy, and wealthy (as opposed to a Demand).

Unknown Territory—events in life that are not known or familiar.

Value—term used to stress the significance and the importance of a particular person, place, or thing.

Worth—the cost of an item when it's bought or sold. **Worth** determines how much a particular thing will sell for in the market.

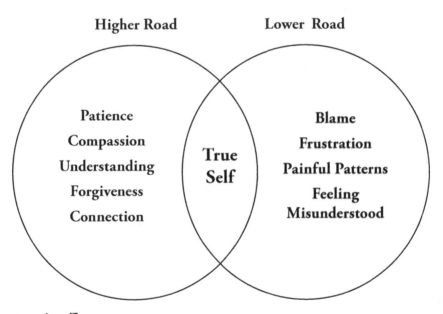

Construction Zone

Construction zones can be a true pain. Navigating them is often slow, and the road can be rough. During this journey there's a construction zone at the end of each chapter. A place to slow things down. To pay attention to the task at hand. To give yourself a movement to connect to yourself.

Funny thing is, we crave for things to slow down at times. We want our kids to stop growing. We want more vacation time. We want to take time to take care of ourselves.

> **Awareness is like the sun. When it shines on things, they are transformed.**
>
> **Thich Nhat Hanh**

Here's your chance. Slowing down through a construction zone will afford you the option and opportunity to deepen your journey, contemplate a few new things, and work with a few new tools.

Here's your first one. Give it a try.

Construction Zone

Time needed: Give yourself at least ten minutes.

From the list of Road Signs pick a word that draws your attention. It could be any word really. In your journal write down the word and begin to flush out what it means to you specifically.

Let's look at the word "freedom," for example, as discussed earlier in this chapter. Using the template below, follow the prompts and insert the appropriate form of the word or the dictionary definition (as directed).

You can use this template for any of the words from our list (or add your own words).

Take the word _____. The dictionary definition is: _____ Now, wouldn't that be great? Just to be _____. But what does _____ mean to you specifically? What does it look like and how would it feel to be _____? The idea here is that if you want to experience _____, you need to define what it means for you.

The more clearly you define a particular word or concept, the more clearly you can communicate it and create it.

Spend a few minutes writing in your journal what this word or concept looks like, feels like (emotionally and physically), and how it would be for this to be a healthy part of your life.

Clarity

Superpower

6

OK, I Admit It.
I'm Lost

Sometimes being lost is the best way to find yourself.

LJ Vanier

The Landscape

Navigating *That Lost Place*

The Language

Automatic Writing—a tool that makes your intuition real and valuable.

The Map

Ok, so it might feel like you took a wrong turn, maybe a few. At one point you had a clear idea where you were heading but now you are feeling lost. Not because you are bad or wrong—everyone takes a wrong turn now and then. It's so easy to get caught up in your day—soccer games and birthday parties and work schedules. Soon your day turns into a week, which turns into a month. You are so busy taking care of everything outside of yourself that by the time you find a minute to get your bearings you get the feeling that somehow you have lost your way.

Of course, no one likes this lost feeling.

Fortunately, you have this Road Map. The book you are holding is a Road Map to Your True Self (Remember this is the place where you are the most alive. You can hear yourself. You understand your needs will be met.) This Map guides you along your journey, helping you navigate through those times when you feel uncertain about your life or yourself. By following this Road Map, you will be able to find your way from shaky to solid, from not OK to OK, from feeling unworthy to finding your true value and your true voice.

Note to a friend:

I wanted to reach out because when I saw you yesterday you seemed distracted, tired, overwhelmed, and maybe a little lost. Lost is okay. We all get overwhelmed at times with kids, school, work, partners, and the drive to rise to the top while we are doing it. Good grief! No one I know can do all this.

Feeling lost is so unnerving. Ungrounded. Un-everything. I usually feel like my head is spinning, and I can't focus.

How does it make you feel?

I know you crave to be steady, grounded, and secure but to get there you need to find that inner voice. The voice that only you can hear. This voice may be weak. It may be having a tantrum. It might be weary and limp with exhaustion. But, trust me, that voice is there.

Talk with you soon.

The Road Ahead

When we speak of losing your way, we are speaking about that feeling of over-whelm, uncertainty, confusion, and constant second-guessing. We are speaking to that very deep feeling that you have somehow lost your sense of self.

Let's make it clear—we all get lost. For you, it may be getting lost in your schedules, lost in your personal relationships, lost in the worry and stress of keeping it all together, or lost in the feeling of inadequacy.

> **Some beautiful paths can't be discovered without getting lost.**
>
> **Erol Ozan**

In this part of the trip, you will learn how to navigate through those times when you are feeling lost.

One way to navigate life, or get back on track, is to tap into your superpowers of intuition. Intuition is that inner knowing that we all have, that inner voice that we often hear but commonly ignore. Come on, you know exactly what we are talking about. That gut feeling. That sudden idea. That "random" thought that just won't leave you alone.

Reclaiming or listening to that inner knowing or what we like to call that "inner advisor," can happen easily. It really can. Sometimes you just need a little support, a map to get there, and the ability to tune out the static so you can *really* listen.

Perhaps your inner voice keeps telling you that you need a break—a break from the schedules, from saying yes to bake sales and soccer games, a break from every-one, if just for a few moments. Or maybe your inner voice is telling you that you could use a break so you can finish that project that you promised to finish that was hanging over your head.

But you don't listen

Let's face it, listening to your inner voice can feel extremely selfish. And heaven forbid, you can't be selfish. So, you shut off that inner voice and choose not to listen. Pretty soon, not paying attention to your inner knowing becomes secondhand and pretty soon you get swept up in everything outside of you. Again.

> **Always trust your gut. Your brain can be fooled, your heart is an idiot, but your gut doesn't know how to lie.**
>
> **Stephen J Mordue**

When feeling lost or confused there is an impulse to try to figure out *what to do*, and that is certainly valuable at times. But for right now it's important to know that your destination here is *not* to get out of feeling lost.

The destination is to connect to your superpower of intuition and to listen to yourself and your inner guidance *even when* feeling lost.

Symptoms of being lost

- Poor concentration
- Crankiness
- Spinning or racing thoughts
- Too many to-do lists
- Unable to make decisions
- Messy everything

Symptoms of feeling found

- Calm
- Focused
- Make decisions easily with certainty
- Empowered
- Sure of yourself
- Resilient outlook

Note to a friend:

When you respect your inner voice, others will begin to listen to you in a whole new way.

Where is your intuition? Your brain might be foggy. There is so much outer static that you don't want to try and find your "inner advisor." Well, sweetheart, it's like taking all the back roads adding 4 hours to your trip or just taking the freeway... get that????
FREE WAY to exactly what will feed you.

You may stumble. You may not find your inner advisor right away. But when you do—AHH, it's like coming home. You will feel seen, heard, content, fed, and best of all, energized to do what you love. BEST LIFE, BABY!

Talk to you soon

It's OK and healthy to listen to your intuition.

AND

When you listen to yourself and respect that inner voice, finding it valuable and meaningful, your husband and kids, your boss, your in-laws, and others will begin to listen to you in a whole new way.

Construction Zone

Landscape

The Map

While navigating through this construction zone, you will create a superpower that helps you in those times when you feel lost, alone, worried, or scared.

This superpower will help you find direction and clarity and keep you aligned on your journey to your True Self.

The Road Ahead

Note to a friend:

Super Friend Suggestion:

To find and connect with that inner voice, I usually do some automatic writing. I know, weird, but it's so useful when I want to hear that voice inside tell me I can find my way. I ask a simple question like "what does it look like to _____?" Then I relax and write whatever comes. No sensor. No editing. Just writing.

Try it out. It will tell you about your wisdom and ability to see the next step. Automatic writing gives you the ability to steady yourself in your own way.

Talk to you soon.

PS

If you don't listen to yourself, then who is going to listen to you?

I believe there is power in asking the body to act on our heart's behalf.

Joanna Gains

Directions

Automatic Writing

What you will need:

- 15 minutes.
- Journal, alarm or timer.

  Begin by sitting quietly.

  Relax your shoulders and take a couple of deep, relaxed breaths.

  Empty your mind of preconceived ideas of how things should be.

Across the top of a blank page, write the following:

What would it look like or what would the outcome be if_____?

Then write whatever pressing concern, worry, or question that has filled your brain, distracted you that day, or kept you up at night. Do not ask yes or no questions, but open-ended ones.

For example:

Not "should I quit my job?" but "What would it look like or what would the outcome be…"

If I quit my job?

If I moved to a different town?

If I lost 10 pounds?

If I had the holidays at my house?

If I started a conversation about _____ with my spouse?

If I left my spouse?

If I moved the kids to a different school district?

If I were confident?

If I felt successful?

If I were happy?

This is a chance to ask yourself-

What do I want, really want?

Please use a specific example from your life.

The trick to the exercise is to allow yourself to write, unedited, without pause or question, for 5 full minutes. Do not second-guess or hesitate, just write non stop till the timer goes off. You may have some anxiety about what you write and see pour onto the page. Don't panic. Just sit with this new insight. Your inner advisor is presenting an inner truth. Allow this to be valuable and to broaden your perspective. The goal is to broaden your perspective and *to steady yourself in your own way.* This becomes one of your superpowers when feeling lost.

OFF THE BEATEN TRACK - Advanced Awareness

Off the Beaten Track is a place you can further explore a particular territory. Like any roadside attraction, you may or may not feel like taking the time to check it out.

You may or may not want to explore this off-ramp. It may or may not be useful at this point of your journey. This territory has some more info on what feeling lost can be like.

There are three main points we will address in

Navigating *That Lost Place.*

Point #1 - If you feel lost, you are not alone; we all feel lost at times.

Point #2 - What being lost feels like.

Point #3 - How to navigate *That Lost Place.*

Point #1

If you feel lost, you are not alone.

Yes, you feel alone and yes, you feel like no one else has had the experience you are having. Not exactly and not to this extent, anyway. It's OK to feel that way. In fact, it's very common to feel this way.

Not until we are lost do we begin to understand ourselves.

Henry David Thoreau

But also know that EVERYONE feels lost at some point in their life. Confused, anxious, uncertain, and unsure of what direction to take. Perhaps a loved one passed away. Perhaps your relationship is ending. Or you were overlooked for a promotion. Maybe you failed an important exam, an opportunity fell through, or your life is taking a direction you didn't think it would. These challenging points in your life are crossroads.

We are not trying to talk you out of feeling lost. We are saying "Welcome." Others have walked this path and have survived and thrived. You can too. How you feel is real. There is no doubt about that. Yet there is a treasure here for you.

Note to a friend:

Lonely is a word easily said. But it can include feeling empty, confused, vacant, and lost. No person to connect to. I understand you feel disconnected from what you knew before. I see that you are flailing. This is the place you begin. Lonely and lost are the start of the blog you wanted to write, the photos you wanted to take, the thing you have been curious about, the part of you that has been longing to be found. This lonely place fuels curiosity. It might not be so lonely when you think of it like that.

Talk soon.

Point #2

What being lost feels like.

Here are a few feelings and sensations that you may experience when you feel lost:

- Tired
- Hopeless
- Confused
- Overwhelmed
- Numb
- Angry
- Frustrated
- Anxious

This is normal. Yes, it's inconvenient. And yes, this is what feeling lost can be like.

Point #3

How to navigate *That Lost Place*

Using the Map, you find yourself in the land of *That Lost Place*. X marks the spot. You are here in this moment, in this spot.

You might stomp your foot and say,

"I don't want to be here."

"I don't want to be lost."

"I have to find a way out of here."

Yet there is a treasure here and you can find it.

> **Run With Me: Someday I hope, whatever your It is, you'll decide to shift your patterns. That you'll take your boat of self beyond the sight of land, with all the risk and danger that implies. Towards where the map warns of monsters. To the unknown edge and past it.**
>
> **Helen S. Rosenau**

Shauna Niequist has a great quote about this spot where you have landed:

You're on the side of the road, empty tank, no idea what will propel you forward. It's disorienting, freeing, terrifying. For a while, you just sit, contentedly, and contentment is the most foreign concept you know.

So, you are on the side of the road in *That Lost Place*. But there is a way through.

Navigating through this territory is done by expanding and trusting your intuition.

You'll begin to expand and trust your inner advisor in the construction zone through a process we call automatic writing.

Listening to your inner advisor and using automatic writing is one way you can move from *That Lost Place* to your True Self.

OFF THE BEATEN TRACK - Advanced Awareness
The difference between *That Lost Place* and *Unknown Territory.*

You may have noticed on your Road Map that *That Lost Place* is right next to *Unknown Territory.*

In this part of the trek, you have explored *That Lost Place* and you have picked up valuable tools and treasures along the way. *Unknown Territory* is right next to *That Lost Place* and is just a short-day trip. It is a place that you no doubt find yourselves in frequently.

Unknown Territory is similar to *That Lost Place* and is best described as a place you find yourself when faced with something new. It's not that you are confused or overwhelmed, it's just that you are unfamiliar with the territory.

Automatic writing is a superpower tool that can be used no matter which territory you find yourself in.

Here is an example of *Unknown Territory.*

> Elderly parents. All our parents are getting older. There may come a time when your parents need a lot of help—physically, mentally, emotionally. This can be *Unknown Territory.* There are many parts of the aging process that need to be worked out. Where will my parents live?

Who will care for them?

How do I manage their resources?

And so many other questions.

Completely *Unknown Territory.*

The main difference between *That Lost Place* and *Unknown Territory* has to do with your state of mind. If you are overwhelmed, hopeless, confused, numb, or angry, you are in *That Lost Place*. On the other hand, if you are dealing with something that is new or unfamiliar and are not overwhelmed but just unable to decide or are looking for wise guidance, you are in *Unknown Territory.*

You can use automatic writing to gain insight in *Unknown Territory* just as you can when in *That Lost Place.*

The takeaway here is that you can use automatic writing anytime, whether you are in *That Lost Place* or in *Unknown Territory.*

OFF THE BEATEN TRACK - Advanced Awareness
A meditation on enhancing your inner advisor.

Find a comfortable spot with your journal. Now ask yourself the following three questions. And of the three, pick the one that feels most true for you right now in your life.

The goal here is to use the superpower of intuition to listen to and tap into your inner advisor even when feeling lost or out of sorts.

Question #1
Are you unable to find your way, make decisions, or create a direction?

Question #2
Are you feeling that someone or something that was once part of your identity no longer exists?

And Question #3
Are you feeling that you or some part of you no longer exists on some level?

Once you pick the truest of these three questions, grab you journal and write down how you feel, physically, mentally, and emotionally about this current situation. Here are some examples below, circle the ones that ring true for you. Feel free to add your own examples.

- Tired
- Hopeless
- Confused
- Overwhelmed
- Numb
- Angry
- Frustrated
- Anxious

The idea here is to recognize that your lost self is familiar. The goal here is to use the superpower of intuition to listen to and tap into your inner advisor even when feeling lost or out of sorts.

When you find that you are in *That Lost Place,* your superpower of intuition will move you from shaky to solid, from not OK to OK, from feeling unworthy to finding your true value and your true voice.

And how we do this is through what we call automatic writing. This is a tool that reveals your superpower.

In our Language and Symbols module we explained that automatic writing reveals your ability to understand something immediately, without the need for conscious reasoning. It allows you to see your intuition in a physical form. Automatic writing is a tool that makes your intuition concrete.

To prepare for automatic writing there are a couple of meditative steps that need to be done. Each one only takes 3 minutes.

The first meditative step will enhance your intuition through listening. Here is how you start:

- Give yourself about 3 minutes.
- Begin by sitting quietly.
- Relax your shoulders, rolling them gently to help release tension.

- Take 3 deep breaths, with each exhale being full but not forced.
- Now relax your throat, gently lift your chin a little, soften your jaw and tongue, yawn a time or two.
- Close your eyes and allow your ears to hear all the sounds around you—the furnace, distant conversations, the TV in the other room, water running, the wind.
- Let your body and mind relax into the moment.

This simple exercise helps remove the busy static from your mind and body. It helps you tune into your intuition and inner advisor.

The second meditative step will enhance your intuition through visualization. Here is how you start:

- Give yourself about 3 minutes.
- Begin by sitting quietly.
- Relax your shoulders and take a couple of deep, relaxed breaths.
- Close your eyes and visualize the front door of your house.
- Imagine that you are standing in front of the door, and you are examining it.

What color is the door? Is the door wood or metal? Is it new, or worn? Does the door have glass? What does it look like? What is the doorknob like? Take a breath and just notice the details. Now imagine you place your hand on the door. Is it cool or warm, smooth or rough? What other detail do you visualize?

Now imagine—perish the though—that in this moment, you get struck by lightning. Would you get struck by lightning where you are sitting for this exercise, or would you get struck by lightning at your front door?

The idea here is to see how powerful your visualization can be. Visualization is a useful superpower whenever you find yourself in *That Lost Place*. It is an essential tool on the journey home to your true self.

Intuition

Superpower

7

FINDING VALUE

If you bring forth what is within you,
what you bring forth will save you.

If you do not bring forth what is within you,
what you do not bring forth will destroy you.

St. Thomas

The Landscape

Own your value and others will value you as well.

Language

Worth—is the cost of an item when it's bought or sold.

Self-Worth—a feeling that you are a good person who deserves to be treated with respect.

Value—the term used to stress the significance of a particular person, place, or thing.

Note to a friend:

I wanted to butt into this chapter early. Your own self-value is a VERY relative thing. Some of you are golden and understand all this self-worth stuff already. Some of you may know you are supposed to feel good about yourself because you are alive, significant, important, and deserve to have goodness in your life. You have no idea, though, how, when, or where that shows up. Some might feel guilty for not having it or knowing how to find it. I know, this is a slippery slope.

It does require faith and courage and devotion to ask for what you want and need, all the while taking seriously the possibility that you may not get it or the even more frightening alternative — that you actually will.

Briana Saussy

Self-value is this ambiguous thing you are supposed to have. And by the way, if you have read this far, you have self-value. Even if the concept is a mystery sometimes. I would like you, for a moment, to bring this concept to the front of your mind/heart. Not as judgment, though. Try on self-value. What does value mean to you? What would it feel like if you had it? How does it show up in your life? OK, carry on. I will see you on the other side.

The Map

OK, VALUABLE traveler, we are looking at new horizons and jumping onto the path of self-worth and value.

Let us tell you a short story. *There are two women (The first story is about Addy and the second about Natasha). You are familiar with them, yet they don't know each other. They are shopping and find the exact same dress.*

Addy has a job interview and needs a professional dress. She has the money she needs but doesn't value herself enough to buy the dress she really loves. She ends up settling for a dress that is cheaper and just OK. In the end, Addy doesn't buy the dress she really wants because she thinks that she doesn't deserve to look that good.

Natasha also has an interview. She's on a really tight budget and finds a dress she loves. She knows she needs this dress, and she values herself and that decision. She buys the dress and feels great—AND she gets the job.

For most people, really owning their value can feel foreign. Truly embracing your value may feel selfish or like you are meeting a stranger; it may feel scary. The destination in this lesson is to recognize and explore your value, the value you already have. Meet it. Get to know it. Sit with it. Then you will be ready to really live your value. The confidence you will gain by following this part of the map gives you the gift to choose just how it is you wish to navigate your day by aligning your daily decisions with your True Self. There is no way to take a wrong turn when your True Self is driving.

When you own your value, others will value you as well.

The Road Ahead

How will you know it when you see/feel/experience your value?
You feel calm, like you "can." You are confident.

You feel like you get to decide when you say "yes" and willingly contribute.

There is a certainty and commitment to your kindness and compassion—the way you uniquely give it.

You are able to solidly focus on yourself.

When you know your value, you will naturally treat yourself with kindness and compassion. As you do this, you will notice that others will treat you likewise.

The simple truth is this: *when you own your value, others will value you as well.*

With a strong sense of value:

1. You know where you are headed.
2. You can ask for what you need.

3. You stand up for yourself.

4. You are authentic.

5. You live with integrity.

6. You both treat others and are treated with respect

With a strong sense of value, you know:

That when things around you are not OK, you *can* be OK.

And no one will listen to us until we listen to ourselves.

Marianne Williamson

Road Signs

As we have said before, knowing your value can be like traveling through a foreign land; it's both mysterious and intriguing. You may have noticed on your Road Map that the Place of Value has three different areas of value to be explored.

The three areas of value are:

1. What you have

2. What you do

3. Who you are

More confused? Let's explore each one of these areas to clarify.

Area #1

What you have

Think of how common it is in our culture to link our sense of value with money and material possessions. As in, the more money I have - the more value I have. There is, of course, a slice of truth to this.

We all do it to some extent. Part of how we identify ourselves is through what we have: our home, car, job, art, jewelry, tools, or clothes.

There is nothing particularly wrong with linking your possessions and amount of money with your sense of self, as long as it's not the **ONLY** way you can feel your value. It's important not to let your identity get hijacked by the stuff you have. You are so much more. Your value goes way beyond your possessions, as you are discovering.

What you have is *not* the only way to define how valuable you are.

We will repeat that. WHAT YOU HAVE DOESN'T (completely) DEFINE YOUR VALUE.

Area #2

What you do

Here we are talking about your natural gifts. Yes, you have them. Maybe you are an amazing cook and love to make meals for friends. Maybe you have a green thumb and grow veggies easily then share your extras with co-workers. Maybe you love to knit and enjoy giving hats to the Salvation Army during the winter.

These are gifts you naturally do, and you give them to the world. Everyone has them.

Area #3

Who you are.

How do you show the world who you are? What sort of value do you bring to any given situation in your life?

You show yourself to your inner circles, your work team, and even new acquaintances by speaking your truth and by acting with confidence in areas where you have a special skill. You show yourself by witnessing and observing others and giving to them in your own special way. It happens so naturally that you might not consider it to be valuable. You might say "that's just who I am." Perfect. Bingo. Bulls eye! That is your value.

Can you believe that we often hold back who we are? This might be one of the more painful human experiences—To stop being who you are to make another comfortable. The value you bring to any given situation is when you show up fully as who you authentically are.

> There is a vitality, a life force, a quickening that is translated through you into action, and there is only one of you in all time, this expression is unique, and if you block it, it will never exist through any other medium; and be lost.
>
> **Martha Graham**

So, the idea here is that you are valuable just because you walked into the room.

I know, drink that in. Feel the discomfort. The shaky ground of it....

I'm going to repeat it.

You are valuable just because you are here.

Being who you are.

(Please make sticky notes and put them all over, i.e., on the bathroom mirror, the car dashboard, by the door, next to your coffee cup)

"I am valuable just because I'm here."

This is easy to say and can seem nearly impossible to do. And of course, this can feel scary. You might even ask, "Who am I?" In fact, the idea of just being "who you are" can go against everything you have put in place to keep you safe. All the defenses, all the times you have managed your own emotions and actions so you can handle other people's, all the times you have experienced that it's not safe to "just be me."

Note to a friend:

I'm going to lay my cards on the table. I don't honestly get this value stuff. I understand that what I have is valuable. I understand that if I can cook, speak a foreign language, or fix a car, those are valuable tools. I don't get the value of just being me. This doesn't come from some victim spot. I was never taught to feel anything like this. Honestly, I'm curious.

I know this is where I'm supposed to actually be giving you wise, friend advice, but I truly would like to hear yours.

Tell me how you know you are valuable.

Tell me what it feels like.

Tell me who you are.

Speak soon.

Review

You have to know your value to know you are valuable.

Next steps

Let's get through the upcoming construction zone.

Construction Zone #1

What you have

Landscape

Discovering Value

The Map

There are three construction zones that you will navigate in the ongoing quest for your true self. These zones will help you discover *who you are* and *what you bring* and ultimately will allow you to discover *who you are* is indeed valuable.

The Road Ahead

The goal is to bring forth and claim those aspects of what you have, what you do, and who you are that reflect your value.

Who you are is indeed valuable.

Directions

What you need:

- Getting through this construction zone will take about 15 minutes.
- Journal.

What I have:

Giving attention to your value through what you have is important.

An overall picture gives you a clear picture of how you value your time, your money and ultimately, yourself.

This is your chance to really look at what you value.

Write a small or long list of things that are important to you.

Your computer
Books

Special jewelry

Garden tools

Glasses

Your car

Make the list as long as you would like. The next step is to assign it worth.

Your computer	$500
Books	$400

Writing this out gives you a deep awareness of your worth. The worth of what you care about the most. Trust me, this is part of the journey.
What did this exercise bring to light? What did you learn about your worth?

Construction Zone #2

What you can do.

This is a snapshot and reflection of your resources—your gifts, abilities, skills, and talents that you do naturally or have learned to do.

Here is an example: Let's say you are traveling in a foreign country. You are careful to watch your possessions yet somehow in the hustle and bustle of travel, you lose your credit card and ID. Fortunately, you are able to do something of great value—you speak the local language. You have drawn on one of your resources, one of the things you do that reflects your value.

This is a simple example of how you acknowledge your value. It also broadens how you look at your sense of value. Going from *what you have* to *what you can do*.

There are many examples of this. Here are a few:

I speak a foreign language.

I bake cookies for the senior center.

I can paint a landscape.

I can fix a leaky sink.

Write a list of your gifts, abilities, skills, and talents that bring a sense of value to your life.

_____

_____

_____

This is what I do that is an expression of my value:

_____

_____

_____

Your creativity, no matter how it looks, is an expression of your value.

Construction Zone #3

Who you are.

Out beyond the areas of *what you have* and *what you can* do lies the mysterious land of *who you are*. In this part of your journey, you are tasked with owning that piece of yourself that holds your value. Here you have the freedom to own those qualities without anyone, even your own inner critical voice, denying their existence.

Circle at least six words that best describe your value.

Loyal	Courageous	Responsible
Compassion	Resourceful	Kind
Empathetic	Generous	Creative
Loving	Passionate	Honest
Honorable	Resilient	Dependable
Committed	Open-minded	

Now write them in your journal and on a sticky note and put the list somewhere where you can see the words. This allows you to claim your value. The story of who you are.

Your power in transformation begins with what you have and who you are. As you prepare to take a journey, you must look at the tools you have, the skills you have picked up along the way, your talents, curiosities, and gifts. The only other thing you can truly bring with you on the journey is who you are, those parts of you that were given to you at birth—your memories, perceptions, beliefs, your heart, and your soul. Knowing what gifts and flaws you are bringing with you gives you the strength you need to know you do not have to be perfect or perform. You come as you are, with what you have.

Valuable

Superpower

8

SIGNS AND SIGNALS

AKA

THE BODY-MIND CONNECTION

Every significant vital sign—
body temperature, heart rate, oxygen consumption,
hormone level, brain activity, and so on—
alters the moment you decide to do anything…
decisions are signals telling your body, mind,
and environment to move in a certain direction.

DEEPAK CHOPRA

The Landscape

Listening to your body

Language

Body-Mind Connection: Your mind affects your body, and your body affects your mind.

Note to a friend:

I know you will roll your eyes at this next statement:

BREATHE

Seriously, just do it. Relax your belly and breathe in.

There ya go. On the phone I could hear the tension in your voice. I also heard the sounds of your very full life—dog barking, kids running in the house and ignoring your irritated "stop running in the house." I think you mentioned that your neighbors had some sort of party last night. Good grief! I would be tense too. I can almost feel the knots in your stomach, fast heart rate, and see your pursed lips. The good news is that your body is giving you much valuable information.

Listen to it! Really. Listen. These are messages that you need to pay attention to.

Why? Because the signals are cues to your wholeness. Does that mean you won't get irritated? Nope. Does it mean that you won't yell? Nope. But let me tell you—it's so eye- opening to know that your body knows.

Speak soon.

The Road Ahead

Have you ever been at an intersection and didn't know which way to turn? Or you followed Google maps and found yourself really lost?

What did that feel like? Did you feel insecure, scared, or anxious? Did your breathing stop and your belly get tight? Sweaty palms, racing thoughts, and a red-hot face may also be part of this.

Your body can give you a wealth of cues and signals that are remarkably revealing and in fact very empowering—so long as you pay attention to them. It's just like when your engine light comes on or your car makes a grinding sound. Something is going on, and it's best to pay attention to it before your vehicle (aka you) starts to smoke and has a total meltdown.

> **I let my body talk, naturally, independently, like a good friend I've known for years who I trust and share the adventure of life with.**
>
> **Alain Bremond-Torrent**

Road Signs

What is the body-mind connection?

Simply said, your mind affects your body, and your body affects your mind.

The body-mind connection means that your thoughts, feelings, beliefs, and attitudes that you have picked up along the way can positively—or negatively—affect how you feel physically.

> **Your mind affects your body, and your body affects your mind.**

For example, the smell of fresh baked cookies causes you to smile, you notice that your body relaxes, your breathing slows, your belly softens, and your shoulders drop. You relax because that cookie smell reminds you of your grandmother who was always there for you in a kind and loving way.

And vice versa. How you feel physically can affect your thoughts and emotions. It's pretty common to be cranky and short tempered when you have a headache.

When you feel physically bad it can even affect how you treat or talk to yourself. Let's say you strained a muscle in your back and couldn't get off the couch for a day. What emotions do you feel? Perhaps you feel worthless because you can't do the things you normally do. Maybe you feel frustrated or even angry at yourself.

These are everyday examples of the body-mind connection.

These body-mind signals include:

- physical sensations
- emotional feelings
- mental scripts

The body-mind signals can be both unpleasant and pleasant.

Unpleasant physical sensations can include:
Tension, breath holding, head pressure, or a knot in your gut.

Pleasurable sensations can include:
Feeling comfortable, relaxed breathing, feeling grounded, and focused.

Emotional feelings can range from:
Worry, anxiety, and overwhelm to confident, secure, present, and engaged.

Mental scripts are the things we tell ourselves. Again, the range is from:
"You're no good, you're lazy, get yourself together" to
"Nice job, you can do it, I believe in you."

Let's take a pause right here, slow things down so you can really take in this passing scenery.

Did you notice that when you read, "you're no good, you're lazy, get yourself together" it felt different than when you read, "nice job, you can do it, I believe in you?" If so, that is what we mean by the body-mind connection. If you didn't notice anything, that's OK. This may be new territory and take a bit of getting used to.

Your body sensations, your emotions, and your mental scripts are not problems but useful signals.

It's totally understandable that unpleasant body sensations, emotions, and thoughts can be so overwhelming that you have to push them aside just to get through the day. And come to think of it, how common is it for you to push away or deny yourself pleasant sensations, feelings, or positive thoughts? The destination here is to begin to notice these body sensations, emotions, and mental scripts not as problems but as useful signals.

Note to a friend:

What is useful about having a knot in your stomach? It's giving you a message. Maybe not a message you want to hear but a message just the same. The knot is telling you something.

You know that your body is reacting to stress.

It's your flashing indicator light on the dashboard of your car. This is your body's way of telling you that something needs attention.

Are you going to ignore it? Or will you listen to yourself? The choice is yours. Ignoring it will give you the same result you have always had.

Listening to yourself—there's the key. The treasure. The power of knowing yourself. Your true self.

Of course, knowing how to listen to your body doesn't mean you won't have another hard conversation and you won't get another knot in your stomach.

There are a lot of hard moments in the world, but your body will guide you, and you do have the ability to pay attention to yourself. Being the truest version of yourself is so important.

Speak soon.

Paying attention to the body-mind connection gives you the ability to choose the higher road when you are faced with any situation.

Or not. It's really all about the awareness to choose what road you wish to travel down and how you wish to travel.

So, when there's tension, yet again, and you are frustrated, yet again, and you notice your blood pressure is up and your head is full, and you are about to yell—congratulations. You are paying attention to the signals your body-mind connection is telling you. And believe it or not this awareness can offer you an exit from a familiar painful reaction to a new choice and a new destination.

It's really all about the awareness to choose what road you wish to travel down and how you wish to travel.

How, you ask?

That's what's up ahead as you enter into the construction zone of this part of the trek.

Construction Zone

Landscape

Indicator Lights - Signals from the body-mind connection.

In your travels to your true self, your body is your vehicle.

The Map

In this lesson you are going to become familiar with the cues that your vehicle, your body, is signaling to you. For example, when that gas light comes on, it's a signal to go fill up your tank. Same when your stomach growls; it's a signal that it's time to grab a bite to eat. It could be that simple, yet the challenge is—can you and do you listen to these signals? That's what it will take to successfully navigate this construction zone. You will need to start tuning into the signals from the body-mind connection.

The Road Ahead

Directions

What you need:

- Journal
- Pen
- A minimum of 15 minutes

Your indicator lights

1. Think back to an event where you felt uncomfortable. Maybe a co-worker made a rude comment, your mother-in-law was cranky towards you, or someone cut in front of you in line at the store.

2. Write a few brief sentences about the scenario. The time, the weather, what you were wearing, what the day was like.

Wishing you a heart open enough to stay curious, Strong enough to face pain, And brave enough to feel joy.

Brene Brown

3. Then, remember what your body sensations were. Maybe you are going through some of the same sensations right now just remembering the scene. Write them down.

Write the body sensations that you usually feel when in a perceived stressful situation. Such as:

Body sensations	Mind / Emotion Signals
Sweaty palms	Racing thoughts
Sweaty armpits	Lack of focus
Pressure in your head	Negative self-talk
Knots in stomach	Feeling sorry for yourself
Tunnel vision	Frozen brain
Tight neck or shoulders	
Holding your breath	
Drained	

_____

_____

_____

_____

These sensations are your indicator lights. When the check engine light comes on there is a feeling of not being safe. The same thing is true for these sensations in your body.

In this section of the journey, you are just identifying the signals. You are getting valuable information.

The treasure is on this road to the True Self is that you have a choice—to know that you don't have to ignore yourself, and to know that there are options.

When your signals come on the impulse may be take the next exit. But hang there because **what** options you can have when these signals go off, is covered just around the corner.

Note to a friend:

Got Tension? Who doesn't? The trick is, who listens? Are you listening to yours? Your tension? Are you doing anything about it?

Please don't leave your body idling in this state.

Remember that your mind affects your body, and your body affects your mind.

So, this is a kind reminder to take a gentle breath.

Shake your shoulders.

Take another gentle breath and let the air fall out of your mouth.

Better?

Just sit right there. The awareness of your body's sensations is key.

You must know how you feel to do something different and feel safer.

Can you do something different to be more connected?

There, that body-mind connection is so important to notice and care for.

I hope you are giving yourself some attention, even when life feels like it's going south.

Speak soon.

OFF THE BEATEN TRACK - Advanced Awareness

- Read *Quest – Living an Enlightened Life in the Mundane World* chapter 3 The Body - Mind Connection By Dr. Steve Stroud
- Each morning, within the first 30 minutes of arising, hum or ahhh for five minutes

Self Aware

Superpower

9

FINDING THE WAY

AKA

COMING HOME TO YOURSELF

Taking care of yourself doesn't mean me first, it means me too.

L.R. KNOST

The Landscape

Giving yourself what you need in the moment

Language
Warning:

Your brain might reject the language used in this section. Or your brain might say "this sounds nice, but I don't do these things you are asking me to do."

Pause—giving yourself a moment to collect yourself

Presence—living with what is in the moment of now

Taking Inventory—using a "pause" to check in with your body, mind, and emotions

Note to a friend:

To be honest I haven't made a habit of this coming-home-to-yourself stuff. I'm uncomfortable with it. Maybe because it's selfish, or maybe if I get really clear about how I feel I won't like what I see. What if I don't "come home to myself" in the "right" way?

I will give it a shot if you will. We can be sloppy together. We cannot like what we see or feel but at least we are paying attention. At least we have taken the first step towards self-acknowledgment. What do you say? Are you in?

Finding the way isn't always easy but it doesn't have to be as hard as you think.

Speak with you soon.

The Map

So, you've noticed the indicator lights are on, and your body is sending you signals. You have been pushing yourself, and you wisely decide it's best to take the next exit.

Present is choosing to believe that your own life is worth investing in deeply.
Shauna Niequist

Up ahead you see that the terrain changes. The land is more open, and the road feels more solid. Or perhaps you feel more sure of yourself. Either way, with your road map in hand, you see that you are entering the land of the Found, also known to locals as the land of Coming Home to Yourself.

The Road Ahead

We are going to cover how to become *present*. Or as we like to say—how to *come home to yourself*. The tools you picked up in the Body-Mind section will come in handy as you move forward. Simply said, *coming home to yourself* means taking a *pause* and *checking in* on yourself.

Yes, you check in with you first—not with everyone else—but with yourself first.

Checking in with yourself means tuning into your breathing, your body tension, and your grounding.

This practice of "taking a pause" and "checking in" can easily become another of your superpowers. For these two tools are a superpower that allows you to become present. Having the ability to become present will empower you to choose just how it is you wish to navigate your day.

> **The more you are present in yourself, the more you can be present with others.**

Here is a truth that may feel counter intuitive:

The more you are present in yourself, the more you can be present with others.

Here's what we mean. If you don't feed, nourish, or pay attention to yourself, you won't have the energy to finish your to-do list, let alone be there for anyone else. It's that simple, and yet can feel like just one more thing to do. Even so, try in this moment to take a pause from all the busy things in your head and your life. Relax your shoulders. Breathe. Take this moment and let yourself know you are OK. Saying "I'm okay" out loud is helpful to hear. Maybe be really bold and put a hand on your heart. We know; it sounds so simple (and truly it is) BUT if you haven't done this practice, it can feel foreign.

How many times have you heard this or a version of this and haven't seemed to be able to make the time and space you need and deserve?

The more you do this, the more you will understand that you are valuable enough to pay attention to (There is a lot of brain science to back this up, but we won't go into it now). Yes again, simple but true. As you do this you will truly begin to create a heartfelt experience of safety and presence first within yourself and then with those you love.

Note to a friend:

Dearest,

I know you have been so busy taking care of everything outside of you that it can feel super selfish to take time for yourself but believe me it's okay to take a moment to pay attention to yourself. And it's also okay to struggle with it. Just let the feeling of guilt and exhaustion sit with you. You're not alone in this. We all get there at some point. And guess what?

It's even okay to not believe that it's okay right now.

Speak with you soon.

Road Signs

One of the best ways to become present or to come home to yourself is to *take inventory (yes, just like a grocery list but for your body)*. *Taking inventory* of yourself is what you will learn in this part of the journey. When you *take inventory* of yourself you are connecting into the body-mind sensations that you explored in the last section. *Taking inventory* can be as simple as just noticing that your belly is tense, and your breathing is shallow.

When you *take inventory*, you tune into what we call *the superpowers*:

1. Breathing
2. Relaxing
3. Grounding

Up ahead is the construction zone where you will be able to use *taking inventory* to come home to yourself.

But before you hit that construction zone and begin to *take inventory* you first have to take a ***Pause***.

Sometimes you need to press pause to let everything sink in.

Sebastian Vettel

Here's what we mean by a *pause:* A *pause* is giving yourself permission to call a time out, even if it's just for a few moments. This is about creating a rule that it's OK to take a break and to take time for yourself. (By the way, time to yourself does not mean scrolling on your phone because that is still about everyone else's life.) A pause is not extravagant. It isn't a day at the spa—well, maybe someday, but right now it's a breath or a moment of thought only about yourself.

Giving yourself a *pause* allows you a few moments to collect yourself. And it's a simple and powerful way to begin to show that you value, honor, and respect yourself.

If taking a *pause* is a struggle for you, that's OK. We know you are so used to doing things for others all the time and not taking a moment for yourself. Maybe reading this now is the moment you gave yourself. It's not easy breaking long-standing habits and mental scripts. But the truth is, each time you take a *pause* you will become a better mom, a better wife, or a better friend. Please know that you are worthy enough to pay attention to your own needs. And besides, don't we all need to take a break at times?

> **You first have to honor and respect yourself before you can expect anyone else to honor and respect you.**

So, let's talk about breathing, relaxing, and grounding:

Breathing.

It all starts with breathing. There's an old saying that goes: "Forget to breathe and little else matters." We all know that breath is vital to life.

> **Breathing is your first superpower**

But guess what happens when you hear the stressful news that your kids' school has closed for a weather day, and you have a meeting to go to? You HOLD your breath. When you are stressed, anxious, or scared, you will hold your breath. Don't worry, this is common, everyone does this. It's a normal physical reaction called the flight, fight, or freeze reaction. This reaction happens every time you are stressed or feel threatened.

The problem is that when you are stressed and not breathing, it's really hard to be there for yourself, your family, or others.

Here is the good news—

This can all change when you give yourself a pause and a moment to breathe.

This simple act, above all others, is the foundation that will allow you to successfully *come home to yourself.*

> **Breathe and don't try to be perfect.**
> **Nicole Kidman**

Taking a pause, taking a breath. So simple yet so powerful.

So, in this moment, take a pause. Put down the book. Take a breath. Deeply inhale, gently exhale. Maybe do it a couple of times.

How does that feel?

Relaxing. "What's that?" you might ask.

We all understand body tension. Got a lot of it, right?

What is your reaction when you hear the news that you sent the wrong email to your kids' teacher?

Oh, my goodness, you can feel that, right? Tense shoulders, tight neck, shallow breathing.

You probably hold your breath AND your shoulders become rock hard with tension.

There is no doubt that you carry tension in your physical body. Maybe it's your neck and shoulders. Perhaps it's your low back or belly. It can be any part of your body. Where is it for you? This is very common. And it becomes so normal that you probably don't even recognize just how tense you are. Being tense all the time becomes exhausting. It robs you of much-needed energy, and it can create pain. Simply said, the more tense you are the more tired and cranky you will be.

> **We will be more successful in all our endeavors if we can let go of the habit of running all the time and take little pauses to relax and re-center ourselves. And we'll also have a lot more joy in living.**
> **Thich Nhat Hanh**

Here is the good news—

This can all change when you give yourself a pause and a moment to relax.

This simple act is the foundation that will allow you to successfully *come home to yourself.*

Taking a pause, relaxing tension. So simple yet so powerful.

So, in this moment, take a pause. Put down the book. And relax your shoulders, or your belly or your back.

How does that feel?

Grounding. This might be foreign territory. A place you have never gone.

Grounding is your third superpower

The third superpower in coming home to yourself is grounding. Grounding is the act of coming out of your busy mind and repetitive thoughts. Grounding is a sensation. Grounding is feeling your feet. Grounding is about feeling connected to the floor and the earth beneath you. Grounding is about feeling yourself sink into your seat or bed. Grounding is imagining yourself stuck like a magnet to the earth.

Get yourself grounded and you can navigate even the stormiest roads in peace.

Steve Goodier

Grounding is a practice.

Note to a friend:

I know." Grounding" isn't the word that you might resonate with. But grounding is the word we use to come back into your body. Even if this sensation isn't exactly what you usually experience, it's exactly what you needed.

Think how you're sitting in the chair underneath you—you are grounding yourself. Think about your shoulders coming down from around your ears—you are grounding. When you feel the socks on your feet, you are grounding. When you relax your belly, you are grounding. Whenever you can FEEL you are coming back to your body. You are grounding. You are way better at this than you think you are.

Taking a pause and grounding. So simple yet so powerful.

Speak soon.

Construction Zone

Landscape

The practice of coming home to yourself – Pause—Breathe—Relax—Ground.

The Map

Here you will put the practices of pausing, breathing, relaxing tension, and grounding into your everyday life.

Coming home to yourself and being present takes practice. It takes practice for everybody because, well, everybody is stressed and tense and holding their breath. Life is full, so it's best to look at this practice as an opportunity for you, not another demand that you do something.

How does it feel:

When you are hugging the most comfortable person in your life and you can fully let down your guard and relax? Your breath deepens and there is a centered "come back home to yourself" sensation. The goal of this construction zone is to practice conjuring up this sensation.

There may be other examples or activities that summon this sensation for you. Perhaps it's fishing, baking, or walking with your dog. Any experience that deepens your breathing, relaxing, and grounding is valuable.

The Road Ahead

Taking a pause, breathing, relaxing tension, and grounding are the tools that will allow you to find yourself and to come home to yourself in any situation you are faced with.

Directions

What is the wisest one-word sentence? Breathe.

Terri Guillemets

What you will need:

• There are three 10-minute sections. These can be done individually or all at the same time.
• Journal

Breathe

Construction Zone #1

This practice takes 10 minutes. You will practice what is called an open-mouth deep abdominal breath. You breathe in through your mouth, allowing your lower belly to expand, then gently exhale.

Here is how to start.

Find a comfortable spot on the couch, bed, or floor to lie down.

Relax your jaw.

Place your hand below your belly button, just above your pubic bone. Using your abdominal muscles, gently push against your hand to push it up, and as you do this count one, two. Once you have done this, then pull your abdominal muscles back towards your spine, and allow your hand to sink down. Again, count one, two. Repeat this a few times.

Now as your lower belly is pushed out, add a deep breath, through the mouth. Full and easy. Allow your lower belly to expand. When full, gently exhale with a sigh. Haaa or ahaa. With the exhale allow your belly and hand to move back towards your spine. Repeat a few times.

The time to relax is when you don't have time for it.

Sydney J. Harris

Relax

To fully relax you first need to know how tense you are.

Construction Zone #2

This practice takes 10 minutes. The idea here is to notice your tension, increase it, then relax it.

Here is how to start:

Make yourself comfortable, sitting or lying.

Give your body a gentle shake through your shoulders, torso, hips, and legs.

Take a breath and gently relax into an exhale. Repeat this a couple of times.

Now add tension to your body.

Squeeze your buttocks, belly, chest, and shoulders. Clench your fists and tighten your jaw. Hold your body tight for the count of five, and then let go. Let your shoulders drop, your abdomen soften, and your back relax. Do this three times. You can expand this exercise to include your legs, feet, hands, any part of the body—even your eyes!

By doing this exercise a couple of times you will begin to tune into your body's baseline tension. This exercise will help you relax the chronic tension that is so familiar you might have thought it was normal.

Ground

Grounding - Grounding is an essential component of coming home to yourself.

Construction Zone #3

This practice takes 10 minutes. The idea here is to stop the busy mental scripts, come out of your head, and ground into a solid embodied sense of self.

Here is how to start:

Make yourself comfortable, sitting or lying down.

The breathing and relaxing exercises help set the stage for grounding. Of course, grounding also helps set the stage for deep breathing and relaxing.

Bring your awareness to your feet, to the floor, and to the ground below you. Push your feet into the ground, imagine the energy draining down from your mind, down through your body and out through your feet into the ground. Bring your consciousness to the center of the earth. Grounding is about bringing your awareness and your energy through your physical body to connect into the earth. By grounding, you come out of your head. There is a sinking feeling, a relaxing of the hips and legs, a heaviness that feels as though we are magnetically connected to the ground. It can kinesthetically mimic the dropping sensation one gets when riding down in an elevator. By grounding you feel safe and solid in the physical world.

With grounding, breathing, and relaxing you allow yourself to move from stress to presence.

Get a pack of sticky notes and write the word **Pause** on it. Do the same for the words **Breathe**, **Relax,** and **Ground.** Place these sticky notes somewhere in your kitchen or living space. These are action reminders. Every time your eyes land on one of the sticky notes, you get to give yourself the gift of self-care.

Pause, Breathe, Relax, Ground

Superpower

TERRITORY TWO
Paths of Influence

10

PERMISSION SLIP

*Give yourself permission to envision a big life, a happy life.
Accept your greatness. Don't settle! You didn't come here to play
small or make someone else's dreams come true. You're meant for
everything that's written in your heart, but it's up to you.*

KRISTEN BUTLER

Dream and give yourself permission to envision a You that you choose to be.

JOY PAGE

The Landscape

Allowing yourself, or someone else, to do a particular thing or be a particular way.

Language

Permission [pərˈmiSHən]—To make possible; to give an opportunity

The Map

I know there's a lot to do today, and just setting aside some time for your journey has been a stretch. The struggle is real. Too much to do is the theme of life. Too many things to think about and too many people to satisfy. You might laugh or shake your head at the idea of setting some time aside for yourself. But here's an interesting detour.

Most of us work way too hard at way too many things. Right? We follow these unwritten rules that say we *should* be at every staff meeting. We can never miss a day at the gym. We have to answer all the emails. Good work. But what happens when you get invited to a dinner with an old friend in town, AND you have a meeting with your boss? You have a pull to connect, laugh, and relax for the evening, but there is also a pull to be responsible and hardworking. Can you give yourself permission to reconnect with a friend? Or do you give into the demands of your everyday life?

Welcome, you have just entered the area of your journey called Permission Slip.

Here you are going to explore what it would be like to give yourself permission to let go, to have fun, to relax, and most of all, to trust yourself.

Note to a friend:

This might be a tricky concept. Only because we love to be seen as responsible, hardworking people who get everything done and look good doing it. Do you need to be reminded to have fun? To breathe? To enjoy your success?

Since we were little, we have understood the idea of giving and getting permission. Remember the permission slips you had to have your parents sign to go on the field trip? They forget to tell you in your adulthood that we still need permission slips. BUT we have to give them to ourselves.

Permission to relax.

Permission to receive.

Permission to have peace of mind.

How does that feel? Kinda good, right? Empowering?

Speak soon.

Learning to give yourself permission empowers you to choose how you navigate your day.

Instead of a day full of overwhelm, struggle, blame, and anger, you have a tool and an option to be your true self and walk the higher road. Giving yourself permission allows you the space to listen to your inner voice, to move from shaky to solid, from not OK to OK, from feeling unworthy to finding your value.

The Road Ahead

In this lesson you will go over the concepts of *giving yourself permission.*

What it looks like.

How it helps.

Why it's a valuable tool in your continued journey of coming home to your true self.

Road signs

YourDictionary.com defines permission as: "*The act of officially allowing someone to do a particular thing; to give consent or authorization.*"

You do this every day—for other people. Everything from giving your son permission to ride his bike over to a friend's house to allowing your mother-in-law (in essence giving her permission) to hound you about how to keep your house picked up and your floors clean.

Note to a friend:

If you really think about it, we give permission to other people most of the day. When is a good time to give it to yourself? Right now?

Giving yourself permission to read this chapter? To enjoy it?

Giving yourself permission to take a walk? Sometimes it is the simplest thing that we have to give ourselves permission for.

Maybe you have a presentation, and you know you will nail it. Give yourself permission to feel that success. Bask in it.

The possibilities are endless.

Speak with you soon.

Yes, you are very generous in giving permission to others.

But what about you? Where do you easily give yourself permission?

When you look at doing this for yourself it may look like giving yourself permission to take the time to have a long chat with a friend over coffee. Or it may look like giving yourself permission to be honest with yourself about how much money you really spent on those pants.

Here is where the road gets steep. Here is where you get to answer the big question.

What if you gave yourself permission to:

- speak your mind
- trust your feelings
- give yourself a break, both from the busyness of your day *and* from the unkind things you tell yourself.

What if you gave yourself permission to be truthful, to be successful, or to say "yes" when you want to and "no" when you need to?

We know that the idea of giving yourself permission can be challenging. It takes a lot of courage. Giving yourself permission does not guarantee that you can make everyone happy. (Is there ever a guarantee for that?) What it does guarantee is that you will be true to yourself.

Note to a friend:

I get it. I can hear the pain in your voice when trying to make the decision about taking care of your mother but needing to care for your family and yourself as well.

Give yourself permission to say "No" from your heart. From a place of ultimate care for yourself. I know you feel guilty and selfish. I know you want to give all you can to your mother. I also know how much she drains you and that she truly lacks the kindness you long for. This is exhausting.

I have found through the years that giving myself permission to say no and to make a boundary has been one of the hardest things. I have had to be strong in my decisions AND kind to myself. I have had to give what I can AND deal with the disappointment of others. It's heart wrenching to say "no" when you want to be "'The good daughter" and say "yes." But really, what is the price you are paying to be good?

So here is my suggestion.

Give yourself permission. Write it on a scrap piece of paper— "I give myself permission to care for myself first" or "I give myself permission to say "YES" to my needs in this moment."

My heart is with you, and I am excited to see what you give yourself permission to do or to be.

Speak with you soon.

> **When you give yourself permission to communicate what matters to you in every situation you will have peace despite rejection or disapproval. Putting a voice to your soul helps you to let go of the negative energy of fear and regret.**
>
> **Shannon L. Alder**

Construction Zone

The Permission Slip

The Map

Learning to give yourself permission with awareness and kindness is the best way to navigate this construction zone.

The Road Ahead

Before we get started, we have to give credit to Dr. Brené Brown, from which some of this work is taken.

Our destination is to write a permission slip for yourself. And why not? You often give everyone else permission to do what they want to do. Today it's your turn.

Writing yourself a permission slip can be an easy and effective way to listen to your inner voice. And to be OK, whole, and true to yourself. Giving yourself permission can be remarkably liberating. It is a simple task, and it will help you build trust within yourself.

Directions

What you will need:

- 3 minutes
- a scrap piece of paper and a pen

Write yourself a permission slip:

I give myself permission to: pause, take a deep breath, and relax my shoulders.

I give myself permission to: drink enough water and take my vit C.

I give myself permission to: have fun at my daughter's soccer game.

I give myself permission to: relax at the meeting today.

I give myself permission to: say YES to a girl's night out with friends.

I give myself permission to: say NO to a picnic with my overly demanding aunt.

I give myself permission to:_____.

I give myself permission to:_____

Sign and date

By signing the slip, you commit to the action of giving yourself permission. You commit to taking care of yourself. By signing the slip, it becomes more binding, and you will take it a bit more seriously.

Put it in a visible spot to look at all day, OR put it in your pocket and carry it with you.

Practice:

WE SUPPORT YOU IN GIVING YOURSELF PERMISSION TO WRITE

AS MANY PERMISSION SLIPS AS YOU NEED.

11

I'VE GOT THIS

AKA

REACTION TO RESPONSE

You Are Here

Between stimulus and response there is space.
In that space is our power to choose our response.
In our response lies our growth and our freedom.

VICTOR FRANKL

The Landscape

Taking Inventory to move from a Reaction to a Response.

Language

Reactions are done on impulse, without considering what the end result may be.

Responses are done with thoughtful awareness as to how actions affect outcomes.

Your new soon-to-be-Superpower.

The Map

Grr.

Ever feel that way? Frustrated. The kind where you want to move all traffic, or really tell someone how you feel, or maybe just scream.

Overreact much? No worries, everyone gets there at times.

Welcome to the part of the trek we call *Reaction/Response.*

Being aware of this reaction/response dynamic will give you the gift of choice. And choice is really valuable.

I'm going to repeat that, so you really get it:

IT'S ABOUT CHOICE!

Don't kid yourself. Be honest with yourself. Take your own inventory.

Jack Canfield

Having a choice is having options. It's having the awareness *and* the tools to give yourself permission to be real. You get to choose to have a tantrum or breathe and speak calmly. You get to choose to give yourself permission to be frustrated, or not.

The High Road is the authentic road. The High Road doesn't always look pretty but it's real. On the High Road, you know what you're doing. You're choosing. Even if it's to be angry. Even if it's a tantrum. Or, even if it's taking a pause and breathing.

Having a choice and giving yourself options is the High Road, the True Self Road.

The Road Ahead

In this part of the trip, you will explore the difference between a reaction and response. You will see how being aware of the body-mind connection can move from a reaction (which is conflict) to a response (which is connection, presence, and power).

Here is an example of what we are talking about:

Reactions are a real thing. We want to tap our foot and snap at the grocery clerk when the line makes you late. We all want to draw the waiter's attention when we are hungry. And we have all shut down silently when we are hurt by criticism.

Raise your hand if you can relate?

These behaviors are all *reactions*. You can see how common *reactions* are. We all automatically and habitually *react*. Perhaps you yell, perhaps you get needy, perhaps you shut down. Pretty normal, pretty common. And though these habitual *reactions* are common, deep down you know they are not very useful.

Reactions are automatic and habitual.

So, let's slow down and explore this a bit more.

Think for a minute about the time you were in a reaction.

For example, how about the time someone cuts in line at the grocery store. Or someone honked at you for no reason. Maybe you didn't get credit at work.

How did that experience feel? Was it fun? Tense? Out of control? Were you breathing much?

When you are in a reaction you probably feel pretty crummy and believe it or not that's a good thing. These sensations, these feelings, are a signal that will help you move from a *reaction* to a *response*.

99% of reactions are automatic.

REMEMBER: WE ALL HAVE REACTIONS.

You are not bad for having a reaction, 99% of reactions are automatic. Our reactions were hard-wired into our brain. Reactions are mental scripts that form early in our childhood as a result of our experiences. As children we come to believe that these reactions will keep us safe. And perhaps they do. That's why, as an adult, these habitual reactions happen even before you can think about them. The problem with these habitual reactions is that they are painful and keep you locked in painful patterns.

The greatest weapon against stress is our ability to choose one thought over another.

William James

So, let's explore this and learn how to go from a *reaction,* which is the well know stress reaction of flight or fight or freeze to a *response,* which is connection, presence, and power.

Note to a friend:

Is overreacting getting you what you want? FANTASTIC. But if it isn't, and it doesn't feel good, I want you to know that you have another choice.

And that other choice is a response. A response doesn't make whatever you are reacting to OK. It doesn't change that you disagree with it. What changes is that you can have an opinion AND be grounded. You can be fierce AND breathe. You can be present AND ask for what you need. You get to be fully aware of what you are doing, saying, and feeling — this is a response. Way less violent on the body and mind. Way more in your center. And it leaves you way more capable to make the next right decision.

Being able to go from a reaction to a response will be your new superpower. I can't wait to see you in your power because I guarantee life is going to give you something that will make you want to scream and stomp your feet.

But now you have a choice.

Speak with you soon.

Road Signs

Let's begin by defining what it means to react or be reactive.

Everyone has a different trigger for what throws them into a reaction.

Common experiences to being in a reaction are: feeling stressed, tense, holding your breath, feeling numb, having narrow vision, and whirling thoughts.

And we have all been there (for some of us many times a day or maybe all day long).

As long as you are alive you will have reactions. You will demand that others be different.

You will get upset when they are not. When you are in a reaction, your body responds physiologically, and you become lost, out of body, or hyper focused.

A threat, a stress, or an overwhelm, signals the amygdala (a small almond-shaped organ in the center of our brain) to activate our autonomic nervous system (ANS). Stimulating the ANS has physiological effects: heart rate increases, blood pressure goes up, breathing quickens, muscles tighten, and stress hormones flood our bodies.

This is the classic fight, flight, or freeze reaction.

A response, on the other hand, is when your behavior is true to who you are in the present moment. A response is when you have come home to yourself.

When you are able to respond and not react you are able to process and not be overwhelmed by what is going on. You are able to be present with your cranky boss or difficult in-laws. It's even possible to be present with your tired and out-of-control kids. You are able to set aside the reactive, short-tempered, irritated self. In a *response* you are comfortable and easy going. It feels good and powerful.

OK, that was a lot of info. Here is a short review.

Reaction:

Your child breaks a vase that your best friend gave you on your birthday. You immediately react by getting angry. You yell. Somehow the words, "I can't believe how careless you are" come out of your mouth. Obviously, this just makes things worse. Now your anger has hurt your child. There must be a better way.

> **The truth is that stress doesn't come from your boss, your kids, your spouse, traffic jams, health challenges, or other circumstances. It comes from your thoughts about your circumstances.**
>
> **Andrew Bernstein**

Response:

Your child breaks a vase that your best friend gave you on your birthday. You are angry beyond belief. Dang right you are upset and have every right to be. But you take a pause, take a breath. You are still upset; you are still angry. That is normal, that is healthy. But when you take a pause and take a breath, that anger does not hurt your child.

> **The goal is to shorten the amount of time we spend in reactions.**

Superpower

The goal is not to avoid being reactive (that is impossible). The goal is to shorten the time you are in a reaction. The goal is to use the superpowers of breath, relaxation, and grounding to spend more of life in a response and less of your life in a reaction.

Construction Zone
Landscape
The Map

In working your way through this construction zone, you will identify your unique reactions and practice moving into a response.

The Road Ahead

Again, using the superpowers you have found while traveling through the body-mind territory will help you figure out when you are in a reaction and when you are in a response.

It's challenging but not complicated. With practice, this whole *response* territory is readily available to you.

Directions

What you will need:

- 15-20 minutes
- Journal

Building on the awareness and tools from the body-mind territory, you will learn to use the physical body as an instrument to *take inventory*. The superpower here is connecting to your body.

Here is a two-part exercise that will help you connect to your physical body.

Construction Zone

Part One

Here is how to start: This is the same exercise that you did in the chapter where we talked about presence. As you experienced then, this exercise will help you connect to and release the baseline tension in your body.

Make yourself comfortable, sitting or lying down. Give your body a gentle shake through your shoulders, torso, hips, and legs. Take a breath and gently relax into an exhale. Repeat this a couple of times. Now breathe in and hold your breath, while adding tension to your body. Squeeze your buttocks, belly, chest, and shoulders. Hold your body tight for the count of five, and then let go. Breathe fully. Let your shoulders drop, your abdomen soften, and your back relax. Do this three times. You can expand this exercise to include your legs, feet, hands, any part of the body—even your eyes! As you complete Part One, allow yourself to end in a relaxed state with a relaxed breath.

Ok, getting through that construction zone was pretty easy. Let's travel forward and head into the second part of this construction zone.

Part Two

Here is how to start: From your relaxed baseline that you achieved in Part 1, contemplate a stressful aspect of your life. Perhaps it's at work or a problem with your neighbor. Maybe your kids are having trouble at school, or that argument with your spouse is still lingering. The topic you focus on doesn't really matter. What matters is that you bring your awareness to the body-mind connection. What matters is that you find the part of your body that tightens when you think about this stressful aspect of your life. Don't worry that you won't be able to find it. After you contemplate a stressor, some part of your physical body will be more tense, and you will be holding your breath.

Your body has gone into a fight, flight, or freeze reaction. Remember, if you are tense or your breathing is short, you are in a reaction, even if it's only by contemplating a stressful aspect of your life!

OK, so you have created a reaction sensation—now what?

To come out of a reaction, you want to relax your body as best you can. Drop your shoulders, wiggle your toes. Take a full, relaxed breath. Contemplate anything pleasant that is not stressful for you: the beach, birds, a flowing river. You are consciously moving from a tense *reactive* state to a relaxed present *responsive* state.

Let's repeat this exercise a couple of times. Start in a relaxed state. Contemplate a stressful situation. Notice where you get tense. Notice that you are holding your breath. This reactive state is caused by a stressful situation in your life.

Notice how this tense place will feel familiar, triggered by the thought of a stressful situation.

But let's not stay here!

With a bit of focus we can move from this reactive, tense place to a responsive "I can come home to myself" place.

Here is how we can do that.

As you contemplate this stressful event—that argument with your spouse, past due bills, your demanding boss, or whatever else you think of—consciously relax the part of your body that is tense.

Take a relaxed breath.

You are purposely becoming tense and purposely releasing tension.

You are purposely going from a *reaction* to a *response*.

This sends a signal to your body-mind connection. It moves you out of fight, flight, or freeze. You choose to give your body a different experience. Your choice allows you to come out of reaction.

Not surprisingly, by paying a bit of attention you will notice that your day-to-day life gives you dozens of opportunities to witness and practice this dynamic of mindfully moving from tension to relaxation.

OK, let's move deeper into this construction zone. Let's take what you have practiced and see how to use it in the "real world."

Now, you get to take the tools from the first part of this construction zone and use them in your daily interactions.

Here is how you can do this.

By paying attention, you will notice that when out and about in your daily life, some part of your body—perhaps your neck, shoulders, or legs—has tightened. Almost always, this tension is triggered when you are in real-time, face-to-face relationships with other people. Of course, this does not always happen, but if you note the subtle body tensions that occur as you interact with others, you will be surprised how often it does. Once you have noticed this tension in your body, begin to consciously relax it. This is the same practice you did in the first part of this construction zone. Only now it is happening in real time. Don't worry if you find this challenging at first. It *is* challenging. Remember, you are reprogramming deeply held automatic, habitual patterns.

> **To experience peace does not mean that your life is always blissful. It means that you are capable of tapping into a blissful state of mind amidst the normal chaos of a hectic life.**
>
> **Jill Botte Taylor**

Ok, this has been a lot of information. Let's review the key points.

The goal is to shorten the time we are in a reaction. Reactions cause the fight, flight, or freeze sensation in your body. These reactions are automatic habits and happen quicker than you can think.

Your goal here is not to eliminate reactions but to be aware of when you are reacting and to shorten the time you are in a reaction. Then, to use the superpowers of pause, breathe, relax, and ground to move from a reaction to a response.

Consider how present and powerful you would feel if you could decrease your reactions from a lifetime of habits to only a few days. Wouldn't that be great? Well then, why not shorten it to a couple hours? Then, with the practice that you just did you can even shorten this to a few moments! Wow.

> **Tension is a habit. Relaxing is a habit. Bad habits can be broken, good habits formed.**
>
> **William James**

The response is the grandest of all mindful interventions. To respond is to be calm, centered, neutral, authentic, present, and powerful with yourself and those you love.

OFF THE BEATEN TRACK - Advanced Awareness

Inconvenient Feelings

We would like to pause for a moment and talk about healthy but inconvenient feelings. You know them well.

This is when you feel angry, frustrated, insecure, shy, embarrassed, emotional, sensitive, sad, anxious, or _____. It's when you, for whatever reason, just feel what you feel. But these feelings can get in the way. They can be so inconvenient that there are lots of times when we would prefer not to have them at all.

We call these feelings healthy because there is nothing wrong or bad about feeling what you feel. Even if feeling what you feel doesn't always feel good!

We call them inconvenient because, well…they can be awkward, disruptive, or just tiresome.

So, the question is, what do we do about these "inconvenient feelings?"

Here is the answer:

Look into your toolbox and use the tools that you are now familiar with—Pause, Breathe, and Taking Inventory—to allow you to become the witness.

> **Feelings come and go like clouds in a windy sky. Conscious breathing is my anchor.**
>
> **Thich Nhat Hanh**

Here is what we mean by that. The truth is you are going to feel what you feel no matter how much you do or don't want to feel that way.

Superpower:

OK, so you are frustrated. Take a pause, take a breath, check in with yourself. It may be valuable to say, "dang, I'm frustrated. That sucks: I'm so tired of being frustrated."

Here you are giving yourself the option to be your true self. Yes, even if your true self feels frustrated!

As you do this, you will likely feel just how liberating and how authentic it is.

As you give yourself permission to feel frustrated, you tap into a superpower. The superpower of giving yourself permission to be your true self. Even if your true self has inconvenient feelings.

Yes, it can be that simple. OK, perhaps not that easy, but not as complicated as we make it out to be.

12

THE DANCE
AKA
PUSH - PULL - STOP - NEUTRAL

Life isn't about waiting for the storm to pass...
It's about learning to dance in the rain.

VIVIAN GREENE

Landscape

The action patterns of Push, Pull, Stop, Neutral

Language

PUSH—an act of exerting force on someone to move them forward or away

PULL—exert force on someone to cause movement toward oneself

STOP—to prevent an action or event from happening; to shut down

NEUTRAL—impartial or unbiased; without an agenda

The Map

Have you ever…

- Tapped your foot while you waited in line?

- Tried to get someone's attention?

- Stopped speaking to someone to make a point?

- Heard your child complain, took a deep breath, and listened, *really listened* to what they were saying?

No matter how far or how fast you travel, there are only four actions that a vehicle can take: forward, reverse, park, and neutral. Remember that on this courageous journey to your True Self, your body is your vehicle. So, in essence, there are only four movements, or actions, that you can take as you move through your day.

Let's explain this further:

Instead of forward, reverse, park, and neutral, we are introducing the idea of 4 *action patterns*: Push, Pull, Stop, and Neutral. In the car analogy, Forward becomes Push. Reverse becomes Pull. Park becomes Stop and, well, Neutral remains Neutral.

Awareness of the *action patterns* of Push, Pull, Stop, and Neutral and their role in your relationships will give you the ability to choose how to navigate your everyday life.

Here's how it works:

All too often too often we try to push, pull, outline and control our ideas instead of letting them grow organically. The creative process is a process of surrender, not control. Mystery is at the heart of creativity. That, and surprise.

Julia Cameron

Understanding Push, Pull, Stop, and Neutral will give you tools and options that allow you to be your true self and walk the higher road. When you are overwhelmed or reacting with blame and anger— "I don't know where I will get the money for that," "She's late again; I can never trust her," "Grr, do they know how hard I work?"—you will be aware that you have a choice of which *action pattern* you are using and how it affects your relationships.

The Road Ahead

We are going to cover the four *action patterns* that we all use when we interact with others. We are always in one or another of these *action patterns* (every moment of every day, 24/7, if you have a heartbeat) of Push, Pull, Stop, or Neutral.

We all know people that push on us or pull on us, and we certainly know a few who just tend to stop or shut down.

The language of Push, Pull, Stop, and Neutral may be new, but you are no doubt familiar with their concepts in your daily life.

For example:

Push sounds like this— "Hurry up, hurry up. Put your shoes on; we are late to school!" or "Clean your room NOW—grandma will be here in 20 minutes."

Pull sounds like— "Hey, honey I can't find my white shirt; do you know where it is? I need it for work today, and I'm running late. Have you seen it?" or "Mom, where are my shoes?" You are tired and have a headache, but everyone is going somewhere, and your family wants you to go too. "Come on, you have to go." Ever feel pulled upon?

Stop can often be silent. An example of this is when you give your partner the silent treatment after an argument.

Neutral is a place of no demands or expectations. It's about being engaged but not being attached. Neutral is NOT giving up. It's a place of options, agility, presence, and connection. An example of this is floating on a tube on a gently flowing river. It's like when your car is in Neutral. The engine is running, the car has the possibility to move forward or back or to stop or stay in Neutral. The power of neutral is that you have options and possibilities available to you.

The goal of understanding the *action patterns* of Push, Pull, Stop or Neutral, is to observe the impact it has on your relationships. There is nothing inherently right or wrong with any of these patterns of interaction. In fact, they can be useful at times.

Useful examples include:

Push—When your child darts away from you and you need to push everything aside to get him back.

Pull—Pull can be useful, as in "let's all pull together to get this done."

Stop—Saying NO when you are being disrespected.

Neutral - Someone cuts in front of you in traffic. Your impulse may be to step on the gas, but instead you take a pause and a breath and choose to be OK with it, not letting it upset your day.

When you know these action patterns and especially your habitual ones, you have a choice and a chance to come to a neutral place. You have a choice to take a breath and create a different and healthy outcome. If you are habitually in Push or Pull or Stop, you will get the negative reactions that pushing, pulling, or stopping have always given you.

Road Signs
PUSH

Imagine that you are late for an appointment. If you hit the lights just right, and there's a parking spot out front, you'll arrive on time. Just barely. But the car in front of you is going slow. Not even the speed limit! "Come on, come on, go faster" you mutter, or yell. You lean forward in the seat, grip the steering wheel, and through will and frustration push and push to get that car to move faster. How familiar is this? If you identify with this, you connect with the *action pattern* of Push.

PULL

Now, imagine you are at a restaurant. You had a busy day and skipped lunch. But your friends have scarfed up all the bread. You look around for the waitress and see her a couple tables over. In your mind you try to get her attention, you raise your hand, and cast an imaginary line to pull her attention towards you. She doesn't notice, though, and heads to the bussers' table in the back of the room. You get up and head to where she is talking with other servers. All the while you are pulling on her to get her attention.

Here is another one. You have had a full day and are looking forward to your partner coming home. There is so much you want to share. But your partner is also feeling tired and sits down in front of the TV to watch the news. You just want some healthy contact, so you Pull on him to see if he will pay you some attention. If you identify with this, you are intimately familiar with the *action pattern* of Pull.

STOP

Have you ever been talking with someone and noticed that you have stopped listening? Maybe even folded your arms across your chest, got tense, and held your breath?

How about when your partner comes home, late again, after promising to be home so everyone can eat dinner together. You are frustrated, angry, and give them the silent treatment.

This is an example of Stop.

NEUTRAL

You meet up with a friend for a beer. It's an easy, relaxed chat. You listen and acknowledge the conversation. They do the same. There is no agenda. There is no time. You are in the present moment. This is neutral.

Your child is late for school, struggling to put on his shoes. You could say "Come on, come on; why aren't you ready?" OR You could take a pause and a breath and see him as the good kid he is, doing his best. Your heart softens, and you help him tie his shoe.

Construction Zone
Landscape
The Map

In this construction zone you are going to add to your awareness of Push, Pull, Stop, and Neutral by practicing what they feel like and noticing how they affect you and your relationships.

The Road Ahead

As you go through this construction zone you are going to become aware of these *action patterns* by exploring what Push, Pull, Stop, and Neutral feel like. This will allow you to see how these *action patterns* affect you and your relationships. From that vista point, you are aware and empowered to break limiting patterns and create new healthy outcomes.

Note to a friend:

Let me tell ya, I do this whole push, pull, stop thing ALL THE TIME!! I pushed on my daughter 5 times before breakfast. Pushed her to get out of bed. Pushed her to hurry up. Pushed her to finish her breakfast. Pushed her to brush her teeth. Pushed her to get in the car NOW!

I pulled on my assistant. I told her to have the files ready by the time I got to the office but…no. I just stared her down as she made copies and stumbled to put everything together.

I didn't answer two questions my partner asked me because I was just too annoyed, and I simply walked away from a conversation I'm just too tired of having. I stopped it all.

The point is. I push, I pull, and I stop all day, every day.

Is it fun? Is it useful?

The whole neutral thing evades me a bit, but it sure feels better when I can find the place where I don't have to force it or demand it or just stop talking to prove a point.

Speak to you soon.

Directions

What you will need:

- 15 minutes

Reflect or visualize a time or event where you were clearly in Push - Pull - Stop - Neutral.

If you went to the grocery store at 5-6 p.m. any time this week and there were loads of people and long lines, what was your action pattern? Were you annoyed? Were you searching for the shortest line? Were you a foot tapper?

What did you do when you got into the shortest line, but the checker was having a serious issue with her register? Do you stare at her and say, "come on, come on, come on" in your head until she moved?

How was your breathing?

After you finally got through the line, did you huff and puff your way out to the car? Did you almost hit a pedestrian because you were so late? When you got home. did you tell the story all over again to your partner… or cat?

Visualization of or reflection on your day using Push

Reflect on a time or event when you were in PUSH.

For example: Were you anxious the last time you were late for something? Did you feel tense across the shoulders? How did you react when the traffic light turned red? Did you use any swear words?

Once you arrived at your appointment, how did being in Push affect your interactions?

Write down what you remember—all the feelings, thoughts, and sensations.

Reflect:

What did you notice about the impact that Push has on you?

Did it have an impact on the people you were interacting with?

Perhaps more importantly, is either Pushing or being Pushed familiar? If so, how?

Is pushing something you do daily?

Visualization of or reflection on your day using Pull

Reflect on a time or event when you were in Pull.

For example, remember the last time you wanted your partner to sit down with you and talk about the meeting you had with your child's teacher. Your partner, as usual, was distracted by a story on the news and was not paying any attention to you. All you needed were 5 minutes of focused parenting.

So, you Pull, mentally and energetically.

Take a moment and reflect on a personal situation where you use Pull.

How does Pull affect you?

Did you have a bellyache? Did you feel bad about needing to be heard? Were you annoyed? Any unkind thoughts spinning through your head?

How did being in Pull affect your interactions?

Write down what you remember—all the feelings, thoughts, and sensations.

Reflect:

What did you notice about the impact that Pull has on you?

Did Pulling have an impact on the people you were interacting with?

How familiar is Pulling or being pulled in your life?

Is Pulling something you do daily?

Visualization of or reflection on your day using Stop

Reflect on a time or event when you were in Stop.

For example, when you have asked again and again for your partner to be home by 5:30 for dinner, but by the time they arrive the food is cold, and everyone is grumpy. Instead of saying your typical "you're late again" you turn silent, won't make eye contact, feel tight, and shut down. This is Stop.

Are you breathing? Is your mind filled with a silent dialogue or justifications? Does it feel good or just familiar?

When you are in Stop, is it driven by the idea that you can show just how upset you are? And on some level is it a way that you punish your partner?

Reflect:

What did you notice about the impact that Stop has on you?

Did Stop have an impact on the people you were interacting with?

How familiar is Stop in your life?

Is Stop something you do daily?

A reflection on Neutral

This is the goal of our program.

This road to your True Self is taking one step at a time, building your toolbox and sense of self-worth.

Your work here is to walk a familiar road and to venture into unknown territory. To know who you are and to broaden your sense of self. To go from not OK to OK, from shaky to solid, and from feeling unworthy to finding your value and your voice.

Your quest is to discover your True Self and to experience the love you deserve to both give and receive.

In this great quest that you have undertaken it is vital to remember that the destination is not perfection but authenticity. Your goal is to gain a solid sense of yourself, and to begin to value your abilities.

The goal of Neutral is not to avoid having a reaction. If you set up the idea that you should never get angry or frustrated or be upset, then you are bound to fail.

The idea is to be aware enough of where you are to have a choice of whether you want to be there or not.

Your goal, as is true of all of us, is to have the tools and awareness to shorten the time that you spend in reactions and to live more and more from Neutral.

Neutral is available any moment that we are able to let down our guard, come to our heart, and be present.

Neutral is...

Reading your kid a bedtime story.

Watching a sunset with your partner and not needing to say anything.

How can you find Neutral when you are late to work, and you hit all the red lights? Do you have the tools and the ability to choose something different?

Finding Neutral, is easy to say and challenging to accomplish.

As we move through this course and in this next lesson, we will help make finding Neutral more familiar and accessible.

Review of Push, Pull, Stop, Neutral

Use your journal to record your responses to the following prompts:

- My favorite action is _____.
- I mostly use it with _____.
- I most commonly use it when _____.
- Sometimes I will use _____ to get what I want.
- This is how Push, Pull, Stop, and Neutral affect me:

Physically _____

Emotionally _____

Mentally _____

Spiritually _____

- I notice push, pull, stop, and neutral affect others in this way: _____
  _____.
- I notice push, pull, stop, and neutral are useful in these circumstances: _____
  _____.

OFF THE BEATEN TRACK - Advanced Awareness

Anytime you find yourself withholding or halting the relational flow, you are in Stop.

Read *Quest – Living an Enlightened Life in the Mundane World* chapter 21 for more on the pattern of withholding love. By Dr Steve Stroud.

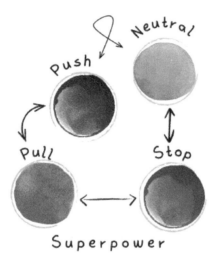

13

FOREIGN LANDS, FOREIGN PEOPLE
THINKER FEELER DOER

Everything that irritates us about others
can lead us to an understanding of ourselves.

C.G. JUNG

The Landscape

There is something quite interesting about people close to you and people you hardly know. What is interesting and challenging, is that they are different from you. And therefore, they view the world differently than you do. Consider that much of your frustration when dealing with others—be it your partner, family, or boss—is that their world view is different than yours.

As you trek through this *Foreign Lands, Foreign People* territory you will find another superpower that will help you navigate the" foreign" land that others live in.

Language

Thinker—someone who navigates life from the mental, analytical point of view

Feeler—someone who navigates life from the emotional, sensitive point of view

Doer—someone who navigates life from the action, get-it-done point of view

The Map

As you check your map you see that the next adventure of the journey takes you into new territory called Relationship Modes. You notice the road up ahead will wind its way over three ridges. Though the terrain in this area does not vary much, the view from each ridgetop is strikingly different.

The three ridges, corresponding to the three relationship modes, are called Thinker, Feeler, and Doer.

Note to a friend:

I know you get lost in your feelings. And that can feel like being held under water. Scary. Like there is no room for air. Your breakup (or losing your job) is the scariest thing. I know you are uncertain and afraid.

If you are able, DO something in those moments of overwhelm. Stand up. Move your body. Weed the garden. Shovel the snow. Do a load of laundry. Move into a routine that requires nothing else but the action. Try that. Or try thinking of how you will give instructions to the house cleaner for the week. What special detail do you want to give her instructions for?

I know these seem silly and mundane, but they truly can help you find a path through the tangle of feelings. One moment at a time. One thought. One action. One feeling.

Speak with you soon.

The Road Ahead

In this part of the journey, we're exploring 3 different points of view. We call them Thinker, Feeler, Doer. We have all of them inside of us, but we are generally driven by one mode.

Thinkers say, "I think that cocker spaniel puppy is cute."

Feelers say, "Can I pet your puppy? They make me feel so happy."

Doers say, "Where is the leash so we can go for a walk with the puppy?"

We all say these things but usually we use one dominant mode to interact with the world.

By exploring these three areas or what we call modes, you will be able to better understand yourself (always a good start) and be better able to connect with, understand, and support others (always a good finish).

> **We each have a Thinker, Feeler, Doer part within us. And we each have our favorite, most comfortable one with which we use most in our daily life.**

Road Signs

Simply put, the Thinker, Feeler, and Doer Modes reflect the most comfortable way in which people relate to each other.

Here is an example of what we mean:

No doubt you know someone who is very analytical, overly rational, and knows all the right answers. This person can easily figure things out and is always thinking. They tend to view the world from Thinker Mode.

You likely also know someone who has an abundance of emotions. They are sensitive and feel things intensely. They often tell you how they feel. They may be happy all the time, or they may be melancholy. Maybe they are just moody. They relate to others and make decisions based on how they feel. Their point of view is from Feeler Mode.

And then there is the person who is action oriented with a driving need to get things done. Projects and a list of things to do fill their day. They usually speak and act like "hey, I'm busy accomplishing things." That person would view the world from the Doer Mode.

It's a basic fact that some of us tend to *think* our way through life, some of us *feel* our way through life, and others of us *do*, or act, as our favorite mode of getting through the day.

The truth is, we contain within us all three relationship modes, although we each have our most comfortable mode. There is nothing wrong with any of the modes. But as we travel this road to our true self, it is essential to understand how each mode approaches relationships.

These modes, as with all our behavioral habits, are developed in the first few years of life. As a child, in response to your environment, you began to understand that one of these modes—Thinker, Feeler, Doer—was the way you could get what you needed and your "go-to" mode when you wanted to feel safe.

As you grow into adulthood, you carry your main mode into relationships, and you will interact with others from that point of view.

Here is an example of what we are talking about:

Do any of the following three questions/statements sound familiar?

Have you ever heard:

"Why are you so emotional all the time?"

Have you ever said:

"I just wish you weren't in your head so much; don't you feel anything?"

Have you ever thought:

"I don't know, he is just so busy, always off doing something; we just don't have any time together anymore."

You have no doubt had a relationship with one of these modes. For example, if you are a Feeler and you are trying to connect with a Thinker, you are inherently on a different wavelength. It can feel like poor reception on a cell phone or radio static—the sound comes across, but it just doesn't land. This "miscommunication" is true for each of the three modes as people operating from one try to relate to people in any of the other.

Here is an example:

Imagine you are Feeler. You are sensitive and intuitive and make your decisions on how things feel to you. Your partner, a Thinker, is explaining to you, for the tenth time, why staying at this one big resort on your vacation makes so much sense. It's got a pool, it's on the beach, it has air conditioning, etc. But you have fallen in love with this little rustic no-frills romantic cabana tucked away up the hill about ½ mile down the beach. It is nothing special, but it "feels" just right.

An argument is looming. You are both right, but you're not on the same wavelength.

No matter how much your Thinker partner explains to you all the reasons why you should stay at this one resort, it just doesn't land. Conversely, making a decision based on a feeling just doesn't make sense to him.

So, the quest becomes how to address your needs as well as your partners. Sounds impossible, doesn't it?

Here is where knowing about these three areas/relationship modes can help you navigate this looming argument and open a connection with and understanding of your partner (or parent or child or boss).

So, consider the possibility that it's not about where you stay. Because regardless of where you end up staying, it's about being able to see from another's point of view. As you practice this new superpower, you will meet each other on a whole new level and begin to sync in a whole new way.

This is the Superpower of appreciating the point of view from each of the Relationship Mode areas.

Note to a friend:

Here's the ticket. No one else in your life needs to truly understand these modes but you. Yes, you become the expert in your own inner world understanding your main mode of relating to any person or experience. If you can understand the mode that friends and family use… BINGO, you have added this superpower to your toolbox.

Understanding ourselves in our primary mode gives us permission to be who we are. This is the whole point.

Life is a mirror and will reflect back to the thinker what he thinks into it.

Ernest Holmes

It's so relaxing to know that you don't need to be any different to make it work. You just need to know the point of view that your loved ones are coming from. It really is like Magic. You feel heard. You can hear others. You feel seen and can see others. You will go deeper and connect.

Speak again soon.

Here is what you would see if you were to observe the different modes.

Thinker

If you were to observe a group of Thinkers, you would notice that they are very mental. The upper parts of their bodies, especially their heads and hands, would be very active. The realm of the Thinker is structured, clear, rigid, and linear. Thinkers process their world quickly and sharply, like the ring of church bells on a clear crisp autumn night. People look to Thinkers to deepen their understanding of, well, just about anything. Thinkers create a framework for concepts and can bring clarity to any topic.

Thinkers tend to be bright, alive, clear in thoughts and impressions. They are logical and can see clearly all the different possibilities to a problem.

Feelers:

When observing Feelers, you would notice that their energy is softer. It is more active in the front of their bodies, mostly centered around the heart. Feelers interact with the world based on the soft, amorphous, ever-changing emotional realm.

Respect other people's feelings. It might mean nothing to you, but it could mean everything to them.

Roy T. Bennett

Feelers process their world more slowly than Thinkers and Doers. Feelers notice what is happening on the unspoken level. They are keyed into the emotional energy that is present behind the words being spoken. Feelers take their time in processing their world, but in slowing things down, what they bring forward is deep, rich, and insightful.

Feelers are open-hearted, warm, perceptive, and can feel others' mood, energy, and even their thoughts.

Doers

The best example of Doers is a work or construction crew. They lean forward, shovels in hand, ready to start with strong backs and shoulders. Anyone with this physical dynamic is a Doer. Doers are ready to lead or to follow as long as action is occurring. Their bodies tend to be dense in the upper part of their torso. They are physically solid, like the trunk of a towering evergreen tree. When communicating, they will often lean towards you to ensure that you are getting the full forward movement of what they are saying. Held in balance, this Doer Mode brings a high degree of leadership and respect from others.

> **We can only improve our own and other's situations with work. We change the world through what we do.**
>
> **Dele Ola**

Doers are active and have a strong core of inner knowing. They see the big picture and can get things done.

Judgments

You would not be alone if you were to have judgments about someone who has a different mode than you do. It's pretty common. These judgments are often formed because you have experiences with a particular mode that was painful. This happens when a mode is out of balance.

As in all things there is the High Road and the Low Road. Here are some of the Low Road actions that can occur with the Thinkers, Feelers, and Doers. The Low Road, as usual, can be painful.

> **To know yourself as the Being underneath the thinker, the stillness underneath the mental noise, the love and joy underneath the pain, is freedom, salvation, enlightenment.**
>
> **Eckhart Tolle**

Thinkers will come across as a know-it-all. They will be self-contained and aloof. They say they don't need anything from anyone else, but they sure know what everyone else should do.

Feelers will be disconnected from logical thought. They become lost in their emotions and emotionally overwhelmed. They may be withdrawn and feel confused.

Doers believe "it's my way or the highway." The out-of-balance Doer is always right and will tell you so. They can be pushy. They believe they are under-appreciated for all they do. They can feel easily betrayed.

Uncovering your Relationship Mode:

From what you have covered so far you may have a good sense of which mode you view the world from, but let's dive deeper into the area to see some more details.

Here are a few questions that will aid your journey:

When you make a decision, what sounds familiar?

1. Do you consider all the pros and cons, researching the options, and talking to people or searching the internet for information? (Thinker)

2. Do you make decisions by what feels right, even if it doesn't appear logical? (Feeler)

3. Are you chomping at the bit to get something done even before contemplating all the variables? (Doer)

How you use your language is another clue.

If you wanted ice cream, would you say...

- "I think I'll have ice cream." (Thinker)
- "I feel like some ice cream." (Feeler)
- "I'm going to drive to the store and buy enough ice cream for the next two weeks." (Doer)

Here is a familiar story:

You probably know someone who is a Feeler. In this story, let's say she was married to a Doer. The Doer husband was always off on some work project or bike race or hunting trip. She desired a heartfelt emotional connection. Though he was aware of her need, he didn't know how to meet it. Had he had the tools and the willingness to apply them, he would have been able to hold his wife (physically and energetically) on an emotional or feeling level. Without stopping or repressing his Doer Mode, he could have expanded his repertoire to include the emotional realm. This would have deepened their ability to connect with each other even though their modes are different. Of course, the Feeler could also expand her repertoire to hold the Doer. The Doer language is one of action. By reflecting the value of a Doer's actions, and by acting, the Feeler begins to meet the Doer in his world. It could be as simple as, "I see that you cut the grass and raked the leaves. It looks great. Thanks for how much you do for us."

The goal in understanding the modes is balance. There is nothing inherently wrong with any of them. With consciousness and practice we can find our way to flexibility and empowerment in our relationships.

Construction Zone
Landscape
The Map

There is a treasure buried in these modes. As you discover it, you will discover yet another superpower that helps you connect with your loved ones.

The Road Ahead

When traveling the road to our true self, we (hopefully) develop a growing awareness of who we are and how we interact with others. Being aware of our Relationship Mode is a powerful tool in helping us deepen our relationships.

There are a couple of roads you need to travel to make your way through this construction zone.

The first road:
    Discover our own mode.

The second road:
    Harmonize with someone in any of the other modes.

By working your way through this construction zone, you can experience what each mode is like for you, and you can practice moving from one to another. We like to call it *Expanding Your Repertoire*, and it will empower you to broaden your understanding of others and deepen your sense of self.

Directions

What you need:

What you will need:

- 12 minutes
- Journal

Destination:

To begin to understand these Relationship Modes in yourself and then to see them in others.

Let's start with Thinkers

To move into the Thinker realm, open and relax your throat.

Visualize clarity and the unfolding of events in a linear fashion: First A, then B, then C. 1 + 1 = 2. 2 + 2 = 4.

> Example:
>
> First, I get out two slices of bread.
>
> I get out mayonnaise, mustard, turkey, cheese, and lettuce. Avocado if I feel really good.
>
> I place the slices of bread on a plate and add the mayo and mustard first to each slice.
>
> I then add cheese, turkey, and lettuce.
>
> I close the sandwich and cut it in half.
>
> Mmm...so good.

Thinkers are "bright" because the spark and activity in their mental body generates a lot of energy. Hold in your consciousness brightness, clarity, order, and a stepwise progression.

"I can figure it out," is a useful mantra.

As you do this, your mind becomes clear. Your consciousness becomes contemplative.

Now let's explore Feelers

To move into Feeler Mode, start by moving your thoughts into the soft, vulnerable aspects of your physical and emotional body centered at our heart.

Energy follows thought. As you open your heart, you automatically move into the Feeler realm.

One way to open your heart is to hold someone or something you love in your thoughts. Take your time. It could be a grandchild, your daughter, or your dog. When you feel a softening or even a pressure in your chest, you know you are on track. As you do this, things actually feel as though they have slowed down. A useful mantra for the feeler is "I feel, or I feel _____". (Fill in the blank). The gifts the Feeler brings to the world are love and care for others through empathy, compassion, and genuine love.

Who would we be as human beings if we didn't feel?

And finally, the Doers

The best way to understand the Doer Mode in yourself is to create action. To do this, create action. Open and square your shoulders, open your stance, and place your hands on your hips. Stand like Superman or Wonder Woman.

You can also raise your hands over your head as though you just scored the winning goal in the World Cup. This will activate your Doer energies.

Hold strength and stamina in your thoughts to achieve your goals.

"I can" is a useful mantra.

You will feel expansiveness through your upper back and shoulders. From this place, you become a leader or a willing follower.

People will give you the attention you deserve.

A final look back before you move on

Some of us think our way through life, others feel, and still others are do/action oriented.

Understanding ourselves in our primary mode gives us permission to be who we are. For example, if you make decisions and relate to others from the Feeler Mode, you are able to take the demand off yourself that you should be different. What a relief.

You know and can practice seeing others from their point of view. As you do this you are empowered to relate to others by meeting them in their primary mode. They feel heard, seen, and acknowledged. Deeper contact with self and others is the treasure you have acquired.

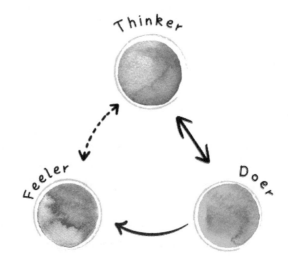

14

LAND OF YES, LAND OF NO

Our inner resources are limitless when they are held strong
by good walls and good boundaries.

BRIANA SAUSSY

The Landscape

Saying YES when you want to and NO when you need to.

> **Before I built a wall I'd ask to know**
> **What I was walling in or walling out.**
>
> **Robert Frost**

Language

Boundary—something that indicates or fixes a limit or extent.

Note to a friend:

No, really. Say it out loud.

"I can say Yes when I want to and No when I need to."

Maybe write it down in your journal or on a sticky note and put it on the dashboard of your car.

I want to tell you loud and clear that boundaries are important. I know. You know this already, but how, you might ask, do I hold them? It's so uncomfortable and awkward trying to say No, but Yes falls out of my mouth yet again. I get it.

Speak to you soon.

The Map

The truth is:

Creating healthy boundaries and being able to say YES when you want to and NO when you need to will, literally, set you free.

Creating healthy boundaries will allow you to go from shaky to solid, from not OK to OK, from feeling unworthy to finding your value and your voice.

Creating healthy boundaries will set you free.

It's fair to say that we all have boundary issues in one form or another. Issues exist either because our boundaries are unclear or don't exist or they become so rigid and impenetrable that they separate us from the deep intimate connections we long for.

Note to friend:

I heard it in your voice the other day, that voice that says "sure, I'll come to the fundraiser tonight," but really says, "I'm so tired I would happily eat a cheese stick and fall asleep in the shower standing up until the water got cold." You understand. My friend, you have the choice to say No because you need to get some rest. Say Yes to the guitar lessons you have been talking about forever or yes to a date night or yes to absolute quiet (maybe with noise canceling headphones).

Speak to you soon.

As you move through this part of the journey, you will learn how to create healthy boundaries.

NO is a complete sentence.

Anne Lamont

A healthy boundary comes down to one fact:

It is about saying YES when you want to and NO when you need to.

Let me say that again:

It is about saying YES when you want to and NO when you need to.

We are going to just keep repeating it until you repeat this in your sleep.

Of course, this is easier said than done. My guess is that you have been here before, in this territory of boundaries. There's something familiar about this spot on the Map.

By understanding and creating healthy boundaries, you have the option to be your True Self and walk the higher road. Healthy boundaries help you avoid being stepped on, around, or over and feeling overwhelmed, blame, and anger. Or not. It's all about defining what healthy boundaries are for you.

The Road Ahead

Knowing how you define boundaries is an essential aspect in the development of your True Self.

You are going to cover the characteristics of boundaries, with a focus on "personal space." You are going to look at the issue of boundaries and discover how you come to hold or not hold the boundaries you do and how, from that point, you can build healthier ones.

Clear, healthy boundaries are essential to your wellbeing. Clear, healthy boundaries foster safety, autonomy, and freedom.

Road Signs

First, let's define what a boundary is. Personal boundaries are the physical, emotional, and mental limits we establish to protect ourselves from being manipulated, used, violated, or trespassed against by others. I know those

> **Healthy boundaries allow us to be clear about who we are and what we think and feel and to distinguish it from the thoughts, demands, expectations, and feelings of others.**

are strong words, but they are necessary. Healthy boundaries allow us to be clear about who we are and what we think and feel and to distinguish it from the thoughts, demands, expectations, and feelings of others.

Let me say that again:

Healthy boundaries allow us to be clear about who we are and what we think and feel and to distinguish it from the thoughts, demands, expectations, and feelings of others.

To get clear about who you are is to state your opinion or your need. *I need a hug. I don't want to go to the concert. I need childcare tonight. I don't want to dog-sit again.*

To get clear about who you are is to clarify what you feel. *I don't feel that the teacher acted appropriately when everyone else thought they did. It bothers me that you aren't taking this seriously. And I feel angry.*

When we think of boundaries, we usually think of something that marks the limits of an area or separates us from something or someone else.

Some boundaries are clear, like a fence along your property line. Everything inside that fence is yours. Everything outside belongs to someone else. That type of boundary is very clear.

Some boundaries, including our personal space, may not be so clear.

Let me ask you a question: Have you ever had a hard time figuring out if what you are feeling is what you really feel? Or what you *should* feel, or what you think someone *wants* you to feel?

This would be an example of a boundary that is not too clear.

Qualities of boundaries

Here are a few other qualities about boundaries: They can change and adapt. They can be impenetrable or porous. They can be well-defined or confused. They can be rigid or forgiving. It often depends on the situation, the people you are with, and your comfort level in that situation. If you feel comfortable and safe, your boundaries are likely to be healthy. A healthy boundary is when you are able to say YES when you want to and NO when you need to.

In navigating this territory of boundaries, your goal is to say YES when you want to and NO when you need to, as much as possible and most of the time, regardless of the situation.

Let's face it, we live in a world of boundaries. Personal boundaries are reflected in how we define our personal space and, in our ability, to say "yes" or "no." Navigating these boundaries

A healthy boundary is when you say YES when you want to and NO when you need to.

with understanding and insight becomes one of your superpowers on the road to finding your true self.

But, as you know, this whole boundary thing can be hard. One way to approach this part of the Road Map is to better understand how you relate to this boundary territory.

Construction Zone 1

Landscape

Discovering the quality of your personal space.

The Map

Here is a diagram. Which boundary do you connect with?

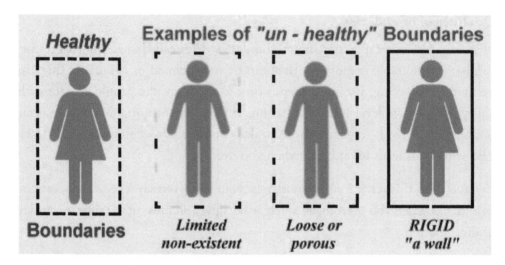

Is it Loose/Porous, Hard/Rigid, or Healthy?

Here are some examples of boundaries. Make a note if any of them ring true for you.

- ____You find yourself saying YES because you don't want to create conflict.

- ____You find yourself saying YES because you don't want to upset anyone.

- ____You find yourself saying YES because you're too exhausted to get into it or make a fuss.

- ____You want to be liked, so you arc the "good one" and just say OK.

- ____You justify being walked on because you chalk it up to "being of service to others."

- ____You feel resentful because others take advantage of you.

- ____You resent yourself for not standing up for your own needs.

- ____You are just too exhausted to deal with it all or to get through the upcoming challenge

If you answer yes to most of these examples, you fall into the category of porous, loose, undefined, or unclear boundaries.

Here are a few examples of the flip side. Make a note if any of them ring true for you.

- ____You feel protective of yourself to the point of shutting others out.

- _____ You feel detached, and you justify your distance by feeling superior or "not needing them."

- _____ You reject offers of help and then resent that you don't get enough help.

- _____ You have to be right.

- _____ You feel tense and never let down your guard.

- _____ You avoid intimacy yet feel lonely.

- _____ You say NO to control or punish.

If you say yes to some or most of these examples, you fall into the category of hard, rigid, and inflexible boundaries.

Healthy Boundaries

All healthy boundaries require one essential element:

Knowing who you are and what you want and communicating that to others.

It's from this place of self-knowing that you are able to say YES when you want to and NO when you need to.

Learning to set healthy boundaries takes time. It's a process. Often the biggest obstacle in setting a healthy boundary is the fear that someone will get mad or be disappointed. Setting healthy boundaries means feeling the discomfort of that fear and then learning to become comfortable with the discomfort.

> **All healthy boundaries require one essential element: Knowing who you are and what you want and communicating that to others.**

Being strong, resilient, and true to your True Self is indeed a challenging task. As you have discovered on this journey there have been some rough spots and steep hills to climb. There will always be uncomfortable situations in life, many of them involving the setting of boundaries.

Whenever these uncomfortable situations arise, take a pause, a deep breath, and relax your shoulders. If there is fear, begin to practice acknowledging it. As in, "Oh there is fear, or I have fear." Allow any fear to be part of you, but not all of you. Give yourself permission to be strong and true to your true self, even if part of you is afraid.

Separate your needs, thoughts, feelings, and desires from others. Recognize that your needs are valid and valuable.

This is challenging and does get easier with practice. Start with the safest people and more comfortable situations and grow from there.

Note to a friend:

There's a space around you and inside of you that's all yours. You get to decide who, where, and when to share this with others.

Talk with you soon.

So, let's talk about Personal Space

So, what does this have to do with personal space? Your physical body is the most intimate of all physical boundaries. We commonly call "personal space," or our "bubble" the place where we feel comfortable being close to other people. Though it can vary widely, your personal space or bubble extends about 3 feet out from your physical body.

The boundary of your personal space, this energetic bubble, is the edge of where "you end and someone else begins." This is where and how you interface with the environment—family, friends, children, and bosses. The nature of the outer edge of your personal space defines how you interact with the people around you. Is it loose and porous and undefined, or rigid and hard? The goal is to first define your bubble and then bring it into a healthy, balanced state.

From the above examples, you should have a good idea if you fall into the Loose category of boundaries or the Rigid category.

Note to a friend:

She asked again if you would watch her kids, didn't she? Darn it, you can say no. Saying no might just be the healthiest thing you can do for yourself right now. I know, I know you ALWAYS say yes. I know. This time, though, try saying no, so you don't come home resentful. So, you have the time to do something you would like to do, like garden, watch a show, or just take a nap.

You may not believe it, but you have the right to say no. Well of course you have the "right", but do you believe you actually can or will say it?

Do you really want to spend an entire week with your in-laws when a couple days would be plenty? Or have you picked up the pieces of a friend's life just one too many times and would really love to say, "No, I need to take care of myself today"?

If you struggle with saying no, you are not alone.

Do you feel bad when you set a boundary? I know I do. Like when I said "no" to my co-worker who asked me to take care of her dog for the weekend, again, while she goes off with her new boyfriend.

How about when you don't set a boundary, and you set aside, yet again, what you really wanted just to avoid conflict or make someone else happy? Do you feel resentful when that happens? I know I do.

Do you feel selfish if you say "no"?

Do you feel resentful if you say "yes" when you want to say "no?"

The boundary to what we can accept is the boundary to our freedom.

Tara Brach

Do you feel as though you can't win either way?

Speak with you soon.

Construction Zone 2
Landscape

Saying Yes when you want to and No when you need to

The Map

Personal Space and Healthy Boundaries

The Road Ahead

Understanding our personal space and creating healthy boundaries is often best done by practicing small but powerful actions. Remember that clear, healthy boundaries are essential to your wellbeing. They foster safety, autonomy, and yes, freedom.

Directions

Getting through this construction zone will take just a few minutes but give yourself time to really think about this opportunity.

1. Make a small list of 4-5 things you want to say YES to.

    Here are a few examples:

    > Yes, to the project at work
    >
    > Yes, to dancing with my partner in the kitchen
    >
    > Yes, to walking the dog at night under the full moon
    >
    > Yes, to the theater tickets on my sister's birthday

2. Make a small list of 4-5 things you need to say NO to.

    Here are a few examples:

    > No, I'm not coming to the birthday party this time.
    >
    > No, I can't manage one more work project and be a productive team member.
    >
    > No, I need some quiet tonight.

Use your sentences as prompts to help you have courage to have the hard conversation, first with yourself, and then with others.

Boundaries are part of self-care. They are healthy, normal, and necessary. **Doreen Virtue**	Practicing healthy boundaries is challenging. Others may not like it because it could be uncomfortable. It takes courage, which you have.

Try it out. Stay in your own space. Maintain flexible but self-aware boundaries.

Get your needs met by **giving yourself permission to say YES want to and NO when you need to.**

OFF THE BEATEN TRACK - Advanced Awareness

Personal space. Defining your bubble.

Notice your breathing and any tension as you play around with the space between you and another person.

Notice your breathing and any tension when someone gets too close to you. That is a signal that your personal space is being violated, invaded, or breached.

Superpower

TERRITORY THREE
Who I Get to Be

15

DEMANDING DETOUR

You don't shackle the people you love with expectations and demands.
You want them to be free.

MARTY RUBIN

The Landscape*

*Warning: This chapter contains harsh and sensitive information for the betterment of your True Self.

Language

Demand—anytime you *insist* someone, or something *must* be a certain way.

A demand says, "if only someone or some part of my life — or even some part of myself — were different, things would be easier or better."

Consider if this rings true: Ask yourself, How many people have to change so I can be OK?

The Map

Here is an example of how demands can play out:

Since you have come this far in this book, you should:

1. Have it all together.
2. Never lose your cool.
3. Always be happy.
4. Be able to speak your truth and stand your ground.
5. Never get stressed.
6. Be there for yourself and for your kids 100%.

Right?

The Road Ahead

 Warning. Demands up ahead.

Somewhere along this trip called life you come to the conclusion that if things (people, events) were different, your life would be easier, better, and therefore more comfortable.

Let's repeat that.

Somewhere along this trip called life you come to the conclusion that if things (people, events) were different, your life would be easier, better, and therefore more comfortable.

A demand happens every time you believe or insist that *you* must be or act a certain way.

A demand happens every time you believe or insist that *someone else* must be or act a certain way.

Demands, shoulds, and frustration all go hand and hand.

You put *demands* on yourself, and on others. And others put *demands* on themselves and on you.

Here are how *demands* can look:

*You may *demand* that your sister be different by not being so dang needy.

*Perhaps you *demand* that your boss show some appreciation, for once, and insist that he show gratitude for all your hard work.

*A *demand* is when you tell yourself to act differently and stop all your procrastinations. (Right now, forever!)

Demands are harsh. Yet how often do we feed ourselves and others a steady diet of *demands*?

A Demand gives rise to a Demanding Voice.

A Demanding Voice is that inner critic you use with yourself and others. It's also the voice you hear from others—your partner, parents, boss, or children.

It's the voice that says:

"You're too sensitive."

"You're fat."

"You are way too needy."

"How hard is it to keep the house clean?"

Or

Fill in the blank: _____ What does your inner critic say?

The critical voice is the one you hear rattling through your mind ready to put you in your place at a moment's notice. That critical voice tells you who you (or they) should be, and what you (or they) *should* want, *should* need, *should* think, and *should* feel.

> *Demands, shoulds, and frustration all go hand and hand.*

A demand is shaming. A demand is expectant. A demand is painful. And that doesn't change, no matter where you run into it—inside yourself, from a loved one, or from society.

See if any of these experiences are familiar:

TO YOURSELF

"Lose 10 pounds"

> Demand - The demand is that you must look a certain way.
>
> Demanding Voice - "Don't wear those pants; they make your butt look like the size of Rhode Island."

"WHY did you say THAT?"

> Demand - to be smart and informed
>
> Demanding Voice - "Shut up. Be quiet. I always say something stupid and wrong."

"Don't be so dang needy."

> Demand - to put others' needs first. Always.
>
> Demanding Voice - "Just suck it up and do the laundry. No one else is going to help me."

"Look at this mess; I'm such a slob."

> Demand - I will be respected if my house is clean.
>
> Demanding Voice – "Get it together. Don't be so lazy." "What the heck in wrong with me?"

"I did it again. I ate chips instead of carrots."

> Demand - I need to be healthy.
>
> Demanding Voice - "I'm bad and weak and make excuses for my behavior."

TO OTHERS

"Listen to me."

> Demand - See and hear my value.

Demanding voice - "You *never* hear what I am saying! You just tell me what to do."

"Be on time."

Demand - Respect me.

Demanding Voice - "Why are you so late? We've been waiting forever!" Cold shoulder, silent treatment.

"Pick up your clothes."

Demand - Cleanliness is Godliness.

Demanding Voice - "Pick up your clothes. Pick up your clothes. Clean up your mess. Clean up your mess." Over and over and over.

Note to a friend*:*

I don't know about you, but I was raised on a heavy dose of demands. In fact, I think all I do with my kids at times is make one demand after the next. WOW. No wonder they resist or ignore me or just plain tell me to STOP!

Do you get this way? Do you feel this tenson inside of you if the dishes aren't done right now, or if the email isn't answered RIGHT NOW?! What if your partner doesn't show up with a smile to meet you for lunch or if you feel you've lost the title of good mom, or that you are NOT a good co-worker or are not in a good mood and you just want your partner to make you feel better?

How do you deal with the demands on you?

Talk with you soon.

Road Signs

Demands create tension in your body. They make you feel like you need to force the other person to get going. Demands create Push in your actions and controlling thoughts in your mind.

Basically, demands create pain.

> **Step away from the mean girls and say bye-bye to feeling bad about your looks. Are you ready to stop colluding with a culture that makes so many of us feel physically inadequate? Say goodbye to your inner critic and take this pledge to be kinder to yourself and others.**
>
> **Oprah Winfrey**

The first step of getting through this harsh territory and these real-life moments of:

"You better show up nice, skinny, (damn it)."

"Know exactly what I need."

"You better like me."

Or "This needs to be the perfect relationship."

Is to simply...

Identify your demands.

(Yes, hardly sounds like enough but hang in there, more to come.)

Once you identify these demands, you can then own them, and decide how much time you really want to spend in this harsh environment filled with demands.

Remember that demands are driven by the insistence that "only if" someone or some facet of your life—or even some aspect of yourself—were different, things would be easier or better.

With a demand you are requiring someone or a situation to show up *exactly* how you want them to. *Always.*

OK let's admit it. **If** everything in your life showed up **exactly** as you wanted it to **perhaps** your life would be easier or better.

But let's also admit that that's **not** how life works!

So, let's not spend a lot of time demanding that it does!

The superpower here is: the fewer demands you have, the happier you will be.

How many people have to change for you to be ok?

Construction Zone 1

Landscape

Demands are driven by the *false* belief that "only if" someone or some part of your life were different, things would be easier or better.

Map

Discovering that your demands limit you and others.

Road ahead

How many people have to change so that you are OK?

Directions

Across the top of a page in your journal write the names of people in your life, including your own name. List all your demands you have for them (and you) under it. Don't edit, second guess, or judge your demands.

> **Here are a few examples:**
>
> Share your feelings.
>
> Love me.
>
> Be honest.
>
> Get real.
>
> Know my needs (without me telling you).
>
> Listen to me.
>
> Be less messy.
>
> Do something with your life.
>
> Be patient.
>
> Be present.
>
> Take care of me.
>
> Be mindful.
>
> Talk less.

Be on time.

Grow up.

Don't be so dang needy.

Drive faster.

Look good.

Once you've written your demands, commit to spending time being mindful about them.

There are two aspects of demands to be mindful of:

First, witness the frequency of your demands. Be honest with yourself. Be objective. Use your journal. Almost every time you want something or someone to be different, it is a demand. Just notice how often that happens. Be a witness.

Second, do your demands have any effect on your body-mind connection? (psst… the answer is yes). How? Tension, holding your breath, headaches, anxiety?

Remember, demands are painful.

Now, please take one deep breath, and watch how your demands are impacting the other person. Can you feel how heavy the demand to be different is?

Bring your awareness back to yourself. Breathe again. Relax your shoulders. You're human. You demand. It's normal, but now you know and understand. You can see and feel the pain that a demand brings to any situation. You now have a choice. The choice of awareness, empathy, and coming back to your True Self.

The fewer demands I have, the happier I become.

Own it!

Superpower

16

OASIS

A place of refuge from the hardness of life

The Landscape

There is a road that takes us out of the harsh landscape of Demands and leads us into the lush and nurturing oasis of *True Needs*.

Language

True Need—A *true need* arises from a place of knowing and listening to your True Self. It's an innate understanding of what is essential to make you materially and spiritually happy, holy, healthy, and wealthy.

The Map

How a True Need can be fulfilled without demands.

The territory of demands can be harsh. When life gets harsh or overwhelming, we naturally want to get away from it. Ahh, but the question is: what road do we travel?

As always, we have the option—do we choose the Higher Road or the Lower Road?

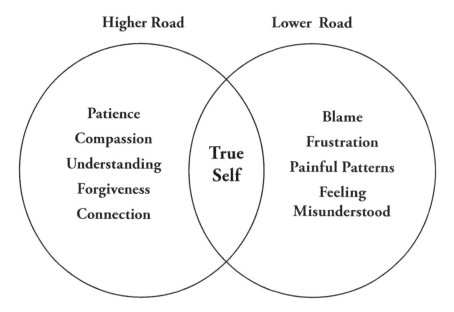

Higher Road **Lower Road**

Patience
Compassion
Understanding
Forgiveness
Connection

True Self

Blame
Frustration
Painful Patterns
Feeling Misunderstood

Is there something you are currently doing that keeps you tethered to the Low Road?

Do you drink a bit too much? Eat the last brownie? Leave physically and emotionally or just don't show up? Do you continually blame yourself or your partner?

Our True Self always contains both the High Road and the Low Road aspects. That is the nature of being human.

Our goal is, by choice, to tread the authentic Road more and more of the time.

When you find yourself on the Low Road (and we all do at times) and you desire to walk the High Road, what can you do? What is the alternative? What can stop a demand in its tracks?

Answer: It's a bit of a secret.

Figure out what you really need, REALLY TRULY NEED and you will soon put these demanding detours in the rearview mirror and be walking the High Road more and more of the time.

Here is what we mean:

The (High) Road Ahead

A *true need* arises from a place of knowing and listening to your True Self. A *true need* is an innate understanding of what is essential to make you materially and spiritually happy, holy, healthy, and wealthy. That's why it's like an oasis in a harsh land.

Road Signs

True Needs are at the core of all human desires. There are five universal *True Needs:*

1- To feel **safe**—being present, checking in with yourself. Coming home to yourself.

> *Pause, Breathe, Ground, Relax.*

2- To be **nourished**—to both accept nurturance and believe you can sustain yourself.

> *Honoring what you have, what you do, and who you are.*

3- To have **autonomy**—to have clear boundaries so you can be creative and express who you are.

> *To say Yes when you want to and No when you need to.*

4- **Trust**—for yourself (first) and others.

> *Going from a reaction to a response.*

5- **Authenticity** —to be real rather than nice or appropriate.

> *This is who I get to be.*

Integration is when you are able to take a new skill and use it as your superpower.

Your body knows how to use the information. You have driven through many territories in this book and have seen new sights as you've traveled this road to the True Self.

You're integrating when you are aware of your breath or the mode you are in (Push, Pull, Stop, or Neutral). When you give yourself permission or create a boundary in your daily life, you are integrating. Your superpowers are using these tools in your daily life.

Note to a friend:

I get it, True Need. What the heck? What is that? Who teaches that? Where can I buy one? How do I even know it if I see it? Are we that addicted to blame and demanding that we can't feel a true need even if it takes us to our knees? We have become so desperate and hungry for recognizing what will help us feel better.

I get it. There is a void. A demand to feel better right now. I'm tired too. I understand how hard it is to exercise one more concept of self-improvement. But this one, my friend, is the soft place to land. Listening to a true need, wherever it is inside of you, is the sweet spot. The fountain of youth. It's winning the energetic lotto.

When we let go of what we think is best for us, we can receive what we truly need.

Anthon St. Maarten

Next time you demand yourself out of bed. Demand your family to clean up. Demand your co-worker to be responsible for the files that were lost, I dare you to ask yourself, "What is the true need?"

Speak to you soon.

At the rest stop...

Take a breath.

Reflect on your week.

Can you feel one of your true needs arise?

Maybe there was an opportunity to listen to yourself. The moment came, and you gave yourself some space to really hear yourself and your true need.

In this example, the experience of listening to yourself is going to fill a different true need for everyone.

You may have listened to yourself, and it felt **safe.**

You may have listened to yourself and felt **nourished.** That yummy feeling of having your batteries recharged.

You may have listened to yourself and felt like yourself again because you spoke your mind or heart **(autonomy).**

You may listen to yourself and felt a renewed sense of **trust** that you can be present for yourself.

You may have listened to yourself and felt **"I'm back" (authentically you).**

The way you experience listening to yourself is YOURS. The True Need that is filled is also YOURS. Listening to yourself was the vehicle for getting your True Need met.

Let's try another example. What about the delicious feeling of connection? The kind of connection that leaves you feeling whole, centered, and like your batteries have been recharged.

> **I want is not the same as I need, and I am doing the following to get it**
>
> **Jury Nel**

When you make a connection like that, you may feel **safe**.

When you make that kind of connection you may feel **nourished**. More like you, whole.

After spending time with a loved one and connecting you could feel like the world is your oyster **(autonomy)**. Freedom is yours.

When you connect with a loved one you may feel **trust**.

After you connect with a loved one you may feel like you are more **authentically** you than you've been in a long time.

Try this with your True Need. What was met? What did it feel like? What did it fill?

Rest in the feeling of safety, nourishment, autonomy, trust, or authenticity. Doesn't that feel amazing?

This is what being in an oasis or at a rest stop is all about (or maybe it's only 5 minutes of quiet in your car because you arrived early for once to a meeting)

Breathe.

Feel how safe you are.

These true needs reveal themselves in various ways. When stated honestly, they can meet the True Need of your heart and soul.

Authentic

Superpower

17

THE JOURNEY CONTINUES

She wasn't where she had been.
She wasn't where she was going,
but she was on her way.

JODI HILLS

Hello lovely traveler.

At the beginning of this journey, we asked the question, "Where do you start?"

The conclusion it seems is that you start EXACTLY where you are.

At your YOU ARE HERE dot in your life.

Now we ask the question, "Where do you end?"

The truth is that you don't. The journey to Your True Self is a never-ending quest.

Our hope is that this Road Map that you have used, worn, tried, turned off in frustration, and come back to in hope has become a part of who you are. A part of Your True Self.

Your True Self is right here. Right now. As calm, busy, and worried as you are BUT with new insight and tools to continue forward into your great big world.

You can come back and see us as often as you would like. Visit any time. All the information will be here to remind you how whole and worthwhile you are.

Superpowers? What did you just do?

You transformed. You grew, and now you are more than you have ever been before.

You're in a place you've never been. How exciting.

BUT life is a continual quest. As long as your heart beats you have a journey before you that will be sometimes easy, sometimes unexpected, sometimes tragic, sometimes relieving. No matter the terrain, you have new skills to use so you can find your one true superpower—Your True Self.

TO COME HOME TO YOURSELF

May all that is unforgiven in you,
Be released.
May your fears yield
Their deepest tranquilities.
May all that is unlived in you,
Blossom into a future,
Graced with love.

JOHN O'DONOHUE

At the end of the road.

> *You have been walking through your wild lands and weaving your own best sense of what is needed and required, right here and right now, into what is possible and good and necessary. You have been weaving the blessings in and out of your own broken places, weaving the everyday directly into the extraordinary.*

BRIANA SAUSSY

Note to a friend*:*

It's so good to see you at this point, at the end but the beginning of it all. You will hit bumps in the road. Maybe even five more times today after you read this. Kids screaming. Work calls you in on Saturday night. I love that you made it this far, and I know you will take this journey forward with you, to places where there are no maps yet. Especially through the unexpected life turns because you can count on yourself. Your superpower is YOU.

Blessings along the way.

Thank you for the journey.

It's been an honor sharing this time with you.

18

WHO I GET TO BE

Follow your heart,
listen to your inner voice,
stop caring about what others think.

ROY T. BENNETT

Be who you are and say what you feel,
because those who mind don't matter,
and those who matter don't mind.

BERNARD M. BARUCH

Your life will give you a range of circumstances, from itchy hives to laughing so hard you cry, from cuddling to getting fired, from computer malfunctions to a beautiful sunset with a loved one.

Now that you have traveled this journey you have a host of new superpowers for every one of the moments that you live. They come in handy for the hard, overwhelming moments.

These superpowers allow you to be your true self more and more of the time.

These superpowers, combined with all of life's moments, allow you to ask (and answer!) the following question:

Who do I get to be?

When the pain of life washes over you, or when you are celebrating one of life's loving moments this question can place you right in the center of your true self.

Who do I get to be?

This question, even though it's so simple, gives you a choice.

And having a choice IS the most super of all the superpowers.

Our True Self is a combination of both the High Road and the Low Road. Traveling the High Road feels better than traveling the Low Road, yet it can be harder.

The proverbial Low Road is filled with the choices that you have always made. Some painful habits (e.g., Like shutting down any time you don't get your way) will happen automatically. You will habitually and automatically find yourself on the Low Road. The quirk is you know this isn't the best solution, but it feels familiar and therefore good at the moment.

However, going down the Low Road **by choice** can be just as valid/valuable/enlightening/empowering as going down the High Road.

Why? Because being human is a combination of both the High Road and the Low Road. You will get frustrated, you will blame. So, take the frustration and make it a choice. OK. I'm going to be frustrated! My choice. I'm empowered to choose to be frustrated. Which means, when the time comes, you can choose *not* to be frustrated.

OK, for the next 10 minutes I will blame everything on anyone in this house! Then, at some point, I choose *not* to blame everyone else for *my life*.

That choice, above all others, allows you to live as your True Self.

"By choice" is not by habit. "By choice" is a response, not a reaction. "By choice" is being present.

Your choice. That sense of self, and your superpowers, allows you to answer -

Who do I get to be?

Of course, the High Road beckons us forward. Always.

Our True Self is a combination of both the High Road and the Low Road.

Traveling the High Road **feels better** than traveling the Low Road, yet it can be harder. So, when you find yourself at that fork in the road between the High Road and the Low Road and you are pulled, by habit, to go the Low Road:

Stop.

Pause.

Take a breath.

Ask:

Who do I get to be?

Reach into your bag of superpowers and with courage, heart, and soul (And choice!) step forward into your True Self.

Remember, as always, it's not that *all things will be OK,* but that you will have a solid sense of self and the tools will work *with all things.*

Note to a friend:

As we end our journey together, I wanted to write you a note and tell you that you have all the tools now to write your own story. To draw your own map. To walk, stamp, dance, sing, or however you want to move your body down the path of your own story.

Tell it. Toss around words. Decide. And, as the saying goes, "be the author of your own story"

You can feel. YES, feel your own body and know how that affects the mind. You can watch any given situation and know if you are being Pulled or Pushed or if you just plain want to throw a stop sign in front of their face.

You are fully aware of boundaries, and even if you aren't you will know where one has been crossed or one needs to be put in place.

You can find yourself when you are lost and give yourself permission along the way to say YES when you want to and NO when you need to.

The outer teacher is merely a milestone.
It is only your inner teacher that will walk with you to the goal,
for he/she is the goal.

NISARGADATTA MAHARAJ

You yourself, as much as anybody in the entire universe,
deserve your love and affection.

~ *BUDDHA*

BIOGRAPHY

STEVE

Dr. Steve Stroud has been a physician and teacher of Integrative Medicine, Traditional Chinese Medicine, Mindfulness, Energy Medicine, and trans-personal psychology for over 30 years. Dr. Stroud holds a Doctorate in Naturopathic Medicine and a Masters of Acupuncture. He has advanced training in Craniosacral therapy, Transformational Breath, and Matrix Energetics. For 11 years he was a core faculty member of the Barbara Brennan School of Healing.

In practice since 1988, Dr. Stroud has helped guide countless many through physical and emotional times of turmoil. His work is heartfelt, compassionate, grounded in science, steeped in the healing arts, and tempered by experience.

Driven by the desire to share deep, meaningful healing work, Dr. Stroud became the founder and Executive Director of The Ripple Foundation, an educational organization dedicated to the soulful adventure of self-discovery and character development that empowers our ability to transform ourselves, our relationships, our community, and the world.

He is author of the recently published book *Quest- Living an Enlightened Life in the Mundane World*.

www.SteveStroud.org

www.TheRippleFoundation.org

LARA

Lara's journey began with a bachelor's degree in creative writing from Western Washington University, but it was her fascination with the body's energies that truly captivated her heart. Over the past two decades, Lara has dedicated herself to helping clients connect with their core desires and realize their full potential as individuals. She uses a combination of BodyTalk and Intuitive coaching to help her clients find the balance they seek.

Lara's passion for people and their holistic well-being is reflected in her diverse range of certifications, including massage, Reiki, BodyTalk, and Matrix Energetics. She's also a lover of marketing, bringing a practical and grounded approach to her work.

Based in a pear orchard in central Washington, Lara is committed to helping creative seekers break through their own self-imposed limitations. As a maker of prayers, intuitive coach, astrologer, and translator of energies, Lara weaves together perspectives and makes tangible changes in her clients' lives.

Beyond her work, Lara's passions include travel, art, astrology, and dancing, all of which inspire her to put pen to paper and create something new. Whether you're seeking a new perspective on life or simply looking to live your best self, Lara is here to guide you on your journey.

You can find Lara at LaraHovda.com

Made in the USA
Las Vegas, NV
22 October 2023

79528917R00092